ENDORSEMENTS

"WOW! I have watched this concept grow from a seed to fruition. This book clearly fills a need. David says that the book is designed "to help you make sense of the various perspectives, tools, and concepts about strategy." And it does exactly that. I have introduced V-REEL to entrepreneurship students and they immediately saw its value. This book will be invaluable in business school classes, to consultants, to entrepreneurs and executives, and to all who strive to make sense of the complex competitive environments of today's businesses. In addition, the book is easy to read ... and it is a MUST READ!"

Dr. David D. Van Fleet, Professor and Honors Faculty, Morrison School of Agribusiness, W. P. Carey School of Business, Arizona State University

Dr. Flint modestly describes his V-REEL strategy tool as a "simple, navigable framework that brings the pieces together." His approach is simple, indeed, but it is also powerful. "Think Beyond Value" will help you create solutions and refine new ideas into something that will actually work in the marketplace. Simplicity in strategy. Finally!

Dr. Ricardo Thierry-Aguilera President and Member of the Board, Mexico's National College of Industrial Engineers and Graduate Adviser for Project, Logistics and Industrial Engineering Programs at Tecnológico de Monterrey, Mexico City Metropolitan campus

Dr. Flint presents a strategic approach that is truly the most clear and concise framework I have ever read. In talking strategic planning, simple and impactful aren't the words typically top-of-mind, but *Think Beyond Value* presents a framework that is both easy to grasp and powerful. If you are ready to make a difference in your organization, this is a must read!

Christine M. Hollinden, CPSM, Principal,
Hollinden | marketers + strategists

THINK *BEYOND* VALUE

THINK
BEYOND
VALUE

Building Strategy to Win

DAVID FLINT

NEW YORK

NASHVILLE • MELBOURNE • VANCOUVER

Think Beyond Value

Building Strategy to Win

Published in New York, New York, by Morgan James Publishing. Morgan James is a trademark of Morgan James, LLC. www.MorganJamesPublishing.com

The Morgan James Speakers Group can bring authors to your live event. For more information or to book an event visit The Morgan James Speakers Group at www.TheMorganJamesSpeakersGroup.com.

ISBN 9781683506096 paperback
ISBN 9781683506102 eBook
Library of Congress Control Number: 2017908776

Cover and Interior Design by:
Chris Treccani
www.3dogcreative.net

In an effort to support local communities, raise awareness and funds, Morgan James Publishing donates a percentage of all book sales for the life of each book to Habitat for Humanity Peninsula and Greater Williamsburg.

Get involved today! Visit
www.MorganJamesBuilds.com

DEDICATION

There is only One who knows the true value of every soul and every decision and step taken by each soul. For Him and His purposes that carry eternal value.

Proverbs 3:5–6
1 John 5:11–12

TABLE OF CONTENTS

Acknowledgements   xi

Another Strategy Book…Why?   xv
     Ugly Statistics: Reasons to Read this Book   xvi
     Who Needs V-REEL?   xx
     What Will Readers Get Out of This book?   xxvi
     How to Use This Book   xxvii

Chapter 1—What to Know before You Go   1
     A Brief Review of Strategic Management   2
     The V-REEL Approach to Strategy   7

Chapter 2—The Quest: Seeking Value and Rareness   23
     Resources and Capabilities Inventory   25
     Defining Value   26
     In Search of Distinctive Competencies   28

Chapter 3—Things That Go Bump in the Night 57
What Is Erosion? 58
The Erosion Matrix 61

Chapter 4—When the Going Gets Tough 75
Enabling Factors for Erosion Control 79
Enabling Organizational Operations 83
Prioritizing Key Enablers 90

Chapter 5—Time Will Tell, but Consider It Anyway 99
The Case for Guesswork 101
Asking the Longevity Question 103
Time as a Factor in Priorities 106

Chapter 6—On the Flip Slide 117
Uncovering Value Destruction 120
Putting Erosion to Work for Good 125
Enabling Damage Control 129
How Long before Things Improve? 134

Chapter 7—Onward and Upward! V-REEL for the Win 139
What You Know Now—V-REEL in Review 141
Putting V-REEL to Work for You 147
A Clear Path Forward 156

About the Author 161
Glossary of Terms 163
V-REEL Quick Start Guide 167
Resources 177
Sources Cited 181

ACKNOWLEDGMENTS

The fact that this book exists is an ongoing surprise for me. The path of life that led to its development was not obviously pointed in the direction of producing this work. Nevertheless, the path led here. The moments of thinking strategically about the options, challenges, and lessons of the journey along the route were combined with opportunities to share life with many, many—I dare say, a multitude of—people who are hidden between the lines of the manuscript, but they are obvious in my thoughts and the memories that produced the text. Those people with whom I shared the path in a variety of ways are very simply the reasons why I can enjoy the surprise of producing *Think Beyond Value*. Can I name everyone in these acknowledgments? No. The list would fill another manuscript with descriptions, anecdotes, and chaotic trips down memory lane. Must I gratefully acknowledge some key influencers who moved me forward on the journey? Yes. Thanks are definitely due and must be given for truly valuable fellow travelers on the journey, without whom the story might have ended before it began.

First, if Christine Hollinden of the eponymous marketing and strategic consulting firm (Hollinden) in Houston had not begun suggesting, cajoling, prodding, and doing what she could to encourage me to develop *Think Beyond Value*, the book would not have been written. It's her fault. Wait—if readers don't find the book interesting and useful, that's not her fault; it's mine. It's her fault that I began taking the steps to develop the book. She's been an encourager with excellent tenacity, and her persistence combined with encouragement is much appreciated.

Without listing all their names, the family members who have encouraged and supported me throughout life in ways they may not even recognize or understand are deeply appreciated. Though I am now part of the senior set in the broader family and miss our parents, aunts, and uncles gone from us, the family voices from both the past and present are heard, remembered, and held closely. My voice, written or spoken, comes mostly from that mix of voices that has surrounded me from my first moments of awareness. I am shaped from the context of their lives. My family is too far away from me now in a geographical sense, and the younger voices are not heard often enough by their old uncle/great uncle David, but the family is never far away in any other sense. Thanks for always being the foundation.

The faculty—past and present—of the Department of Management in the Mays Business School at Texas A&M University has kept me humble, taught me well, challenged my thinking, and provided an academic home for me for most of the years in which I've played in the academic world. Boldly stated, without the friendship, encouragement, and sharing of knowledge of those same faculty members, I wouldn't have had the opportunities in life that I've enjoyed. While *Think Beyond Value* is not intended to be an academic text, it has been shaped by the influences of the truly world-class faculty of the Department of Management and the Mays Business School. The collegiality combined with the rigorous research of that faculty over decades has made the Department of Management one of the best places to be in the world for thinking and learning about organizations. I am grateful to be associated with those colleagues of Aggieland. Of special note, Dr. Asghar Zardkoohi's friendship and guidance over the decades is of legendary quality, and not just for me. He is a special creation in this world. There is nothing but applause for him from my corner.

Two other colleagues who are friends of the caliber one should never take for granted are Dr. David D. Van Fleet and Dr. Kenneth D. Cory. The V-REEL[TM,1] Framework would not be what it is without their input and feedback across the years. Period. We have published academic articles together,[2,3,4] but that is a very small and less-than-fully representative indicator of how much they have helped me think… and think… and think… about how to improve and use the oft-times muddled ideas that arise within my gray matter. I shared several years of being a faculty member at Arizona State University West Campus with Dr. Van Fleet. Those were good years. But changes over time and distance haven't diminished his ability to move my life forward by still being part of the journey. I shared a doctoral student office space with Dr. Cory for about five years before he and I had those Ph.D. letters attached to our academic pedigrees. Our paths have continued to overlap in the decades since those long-gone office-sharing days. That's a very good thing. If anybody ever wants a character study on what a best friend should be in life, I could write one using Ken as the pattern.

Finally, though I really could fill another book with bits of written applause to former students, business associates, friends, the faculty colleagues with whom I enjoyed working for five years at the Woodbury School of Business at Utah Valley University, and other travelers along the path to *Think Beyond Value*, I will conclude these acknowledgments with applause for Jose and Joan Quintana. Jose is an encourager of others, pure and simple. His incubation of new ventures and pouring himself into the people of the community around him is unparalleled in my experience. His friendship is an important part of life, but he did something of inestimable importance regarding the development of this book. He introduced me to his wife, Joan. This book would not exist without Joan's work. She took hours and hours (I lost count a long time ago) of conversations, consulting interactions, interviews, and ideas and made them make sense. The book would not be a book without her gifted guidance. Big, big applause!

In the end, as all authors must do, I shall take full responsibility for the content of this book, which includes any errors, omissions, and silliness that inadvertently may fall within the pages of *Think Beyond Value*. But I shall also note that the contributions of Morgan James Publishing company's very helpful and supportive staff, Erin Casey's editorial suggestions, the Fidelis company's graphics, and the mountain of effort that Joan has put into the book's development have all served to create any positive, valuable, and helpful parts of this book. To say this was accomplished without the help of others would be to tell a very big lie.

I hope that everyone, named or unnamed above, who has helped bring this work to fruition by being part of my long journey up to this moment can find a reason to smile because they were along for part of the ride.

Philippians 1:3
David

ANOTHER STRATEGY BOOK...WHY?

Strategy. It's an overused and increasingly maligned word among business leaders who know a solid strategy is necessary but just haven't found the "right" strategy yet—or at the very least, a strategic approach they can stick with long term. Still, if you are like most business leaders, you, too, are constantly in search of the best approach or an easy solution to developing sound strategy that works in today's dynamic business environment. All the effort you've put into studying strategy books, brainstorming around the table in strategic meetings, and working into the night to think through fresh new business approaches is time well spent. And yet you never really arrive at a clear, well-reasoned plan. And therein lies the problem. Clarity is elusive.

In truth, all the ingredients and tools for sound strategy formulation already exist. What is lacking is a simple, navigable framework that brings the pieces together in a coherent way. My goal with this book is to help you make sense of the various perspectives, tools, and concepts about strategy—most of which are likely familiar to you—so that you can think about and form *your* business strategy. What I am bringing to the conversation is a more coherent way to move from ideas, information, and data, to recommendations and action plans. What I am offering is a framework to work through all the knowledge and information that you have about your business and your market so that, having spent time and resources on strategy, you arrive at a place of clarity and confidence. My goal is to prepare you to drive your business forward or, in some cases, stop altogether and seek a new or simply better opportunity.

 Use V-REEL to plan and run stronger, more financially sustainable organizations.

In this book, I'll explain what I call the V-REEL Framework, a simple and intuitive way to think about *Value* creation, *Rareness* in the marketplace, *Eroding Factors* likely to eat away at your rareness and value creation, *Enabling Factors* necessary to make your business succeed, and finally, but very importantly, considerations of the *Longevity* of your organization. I'll explain how you can use V-REEL to plan and run stronger, more financially sustainable organizations—for profit and not-for-profit alike. I'll show how you can use the framework to uncover winning new ideas and avoid getting caught up in entrepreneurial enthusiasm, all the while forgetting to consider factors that, left untended, could very likely lead to financial catastrophe.

Before we go any further, though, let me be clear: V-REEL is not a quick fix nor is it the be-all-end-all solution to all your organizational problems. It is not even a replacement for existing sound strategy tools. But for those who understand the value of and are willing to invest in strategy, V-REEL can help ensure that your investment offers great returns.

Ugly Statistics: Reasons to Read this Book

Years of teaching strategy have shown me that traditional strategy formulation methods tend to offer a whole lot of information and no real method for thinking through all the data to come up with a clear, well-reasoned plan to move forward. Let's look at Master of Business Administration (MBA) students, for example. Having completed the academic portion of a traditional strategy course, students are assigned a capstone team project that applies all they've learned to assist a business in the community. These projects require aspiring MBAs to assume the role of consultant and help the client company solve some problems or form a strategy. The students generally do a fine job following all the standard steps of strategy formulation. They work through Porter's Five Forces for assessing competition in the marketplace, look at internal and external factors, and talk through a resource-based view of the firm (more on these things later). They generally do all the right things but ultimately struggle to come up with solid recommendations for what the company should actually do—or not do—given its situation. My students report back to me all manner of information about the company, markets, competitors, etc., but when it comes to offering— let alone defending—concrete, well-reasoned recommendations for the company, students typically struggle to make that final leap. They have all these tools and methods, but it is a rare student who can think through all the information those tools and methods provide and formulate well-reasoned, defensible, strategic recommendations.

It's no surprise, then, that a recent Bloomberg study, "The Bloomberg Recruiter Report: Job Skills Companies Want But Can't Get,"[5] identified strategic thinking as a skill that is both rare and highly sought after by employers. And unlike other skills considered in the study, strategic thinking is in the "Less Common, More Desired" category across all industries considered. Be it consulting, consumer products, energy, financial services, health care, manufacturing, or technology, Bloomberg's survey of 1,320 job recruiters at more than six hundred companies clearly indicates that strategic thinking skills are in short supply.

Traditional strategy formulation methods offer a whole lot of information and no clear method for developing a well-reasoned plan to move forward.

Before you dismiss the lack of strategic thinking skills as a problem of youth and inexperience, consider how much money corporations spend on strategy consultants, strategic management training, and the like. Executive MBA programs are available at almost every major business school in the U.S. targeting mid- and high-level executives who have an eye toward the C-suite. Often, it's the employers footing the bill. Then there are strategy consultants. Judging by the sheer number of us—as one among the masses I can tell you we are everywhere—it's clear companies are willing or perhaps feel forced to outsource this most critical of business processes. But those same business leaders who write the checks to strategists are the ones telling HR departments to find strategic thinkers.

Also consider those businesses too small to have their own HR departments. Small businesses form the backbone of our economy and yet struggle to survive—let alone thrive—in the marketplace. Perhaps even more than established corporations, small businesses are in desperate need of sound strategic thinking, and they need it to be simple enough for business owners to work through while managing the HR department, being the receptionist, the cook, and the accountant. After all, that's how the vast majority of businesses operate—small, lean, and very likely short on business strategy.

You've probably heard the grim numbers that get thrown around about failure rates of small businesses. The most common statistic I hear repeated has 90 percent of businesses failing. In truth, it's not quite that bad, but it's not great, either. According to the United States Small Business Administration, roughly 50 percent of new businesses, independent of industry, fail before their fifth anniversary.[6] Of course, that begs the question, what are the top reasons cited for failure? Review the listing of Specific Pitfalls in Table 1: The Underlying Causes of Business Failure.[7] Can you see the need for sound business strategy? Every item on that list save disaster could very likely be avoided—or at least managed—if only sound strategic thinking were put into play before the investment of time and resources.

	Major Cause	% of failure	Specific pitfalls
1	Incompetence	46%	Emotional Pricing
			Living too high for the business
			Nonpayment of taxes
			No knowledge of pricing
			Lack of planning
			No knowledge of financing
			No experience in record keeping
2	Unbalanced experience or lack of managerial experience	30%	Poor credit granting practices
			Expansion too rapid
			Inadequate borrowing practices
3	Lack of experience in line of goods or services	11%	Carry adequate inventory
			No knowledge of suppliers
			Wasted advertising budget
4	Neglect, fraud, disaster	1%	

Table 1. The Underlying Causes of Business Failure

The bottom line is that all businesses (except perhaps strategy consultants) would be better off if owners, managers, and rising executives successfully practiced strategic thinking skills for a term well before they ever arrived in the C-suite. It would be even better if entire teams could converse around a common set of terms simple enough to intuitively inform the strategic thought process while offering enough depth to summon soundness of reason. That's what I'm going for with the V-REEL Framework: simple and sound strategic reasoning.

Back in the late 90s, having become sufficiently frustrated with floundering student strategists and wanting to try to improve the situation, I began to form a tool to aid both the teaching and practice of business strategy formulation. After years of tweaking and refining with colleagues and clients across the U.S. and around the globe, I've formed the V-REEL Framework. It is strong enough alone to elicit solid thinking and discussion about value creation. It is also open and flexible enough to allow for the interjection of vetted tools and techniques that can and should inform your planning. However you choose to use it, I believe you will find it useful.

Who Needs V-REEL?

The most natural audience for this book is entrepreneurs—those brave men and women who put it all on the line to bring their passion to life, introduce the latest disruptive technology, or simply keep the family business going. But V-REEL isn't only a tool for start-ups. While certainly those working to devise a business strategy for a new enterprise will do well to work through the framework, so, too, will established businesses and not-for-profits returning to their strategic planning routines. V-REEL will also be useful to product developers preparing to bring something new to market, and it is even helpful for individuals who are thinking through career plans. Any organization or individual thinking about how to bring value to an audience can use the V-REEL Framework to guide strategy formulation.

V-REEL has great potential to provide teams with a common vocabulary. It can assist leaders in facilitating productive discussions, help get to the root of challenges, and identify where limited resources might best be allocated toward sustaining competitive advantage. The framework helps executives and entire teams recognize the business functions underlying the distinctive competencies that enable them to create value in the marketplace. Plainly, no matter the size or nature of your organization, if you're trying to get your team to think strategically, V-REEL is a framework to help do so.

 No matter the size or nature of your organization, if you're trying to get your team to think strategically, V-REEL is a framework to help do so.

The V-REEL Framework for strategy formulation can be applied to a wide range of situations, but there are some particular scenarios where V-REEL can make a real difference in your thinking and plan of action. If any of the following sound familiar to you, then understanding and applying the V-REEL Framework will help you and your team form a strategy to thrive in a dynamic marketplace.

Your gut is telling you to go for it.

Okay. So you've got a great idea, and all your friends nod enthusiastically when you tell them about it. "Go for it!" they say, and your gut agrees. Great! Really, that's awesome... but it will be even more awesome when you've taken the time to think through that amazing value proposition, determine how rare it is in your market, what might come along to erode that rareness, what enabling resources you need to deliver on your big idea, and how long you have before things change. Do all of that, and if you still have a great idea, please, go for it! But do yourself a big financial favor. REEL in your idea first. Look critically at how you might create value and always be willing to walk away from bad ideas.

Your employees keep bugging you with half-baked ideas.

I'm so sorry. You're a busy person. You really need your employees to think things through before they waste your time presenting yet another unoriginal, logistically impossible, and/or financially infeasible plan. I'm telling you, those strategic thinking skills are rare, my friend. *Really* rare. But try working through V-REEL with your people. You'll be surprised how quickly and easily they'll understand the ideas and adopt the language. And then tell them to REEL in their ideas before they ever set foot in your office to make a pitch.

You have a strategy, but it isn't working out as planned.

That happens a lot. Here's the deal: there are a lot of good strategy books and tools out there. You probably know them—the *Business Model Canvas*, *Blue Ocean Strategy*, SWOT analysis, etc. These are good, but there are things they tend not to consider, like longevity—how long do you have before things change? And incompetencies—those things that you need to fix or influence for your strategy to actually work. V-REEL will help you complete the strategy process and consider both your distinctive competencies and incompetencies so that you can achieve your vision.

You know you need a strategy but have no idea where to start.

Great! It sounds like you're getting ready to embark on something new. Taking the time to think it through is a very good idea, but with so many tools and plans it can be difficult to know which is best or where to start. V-REEL is designed for that very reason: to help you navigate the strategy formulation process to its completion, making use of available tools as it makes sense for your situation. There is no one-size-fits-all cookie-cutter solution, but V-REEL can help you determine if you have something that's really worth jumping into and how to keep that something going as long as possible.

You're pitching your idea soon and want to be well prepared.

Good for you! It sounds like you've already done a lot of homework, thinking through internal and external environments, understanding your market, and shaping your value proposition accordingly. V-REEL will help you check yourself so you are prepared to respond confidently to the hard questions: Do you have something of value? Is it rare? How will you preserve that rareness over time? What capabilities do you need to put into place to ensure you can deliver? Don't be afraid to use V-REEL to shine a very critical light on your idea. Worst-case scenario, you realize it's not such a good idea after all; you avoid a lot of heartache and free yourself up to pursue something better.

Whether you're working within an established enterprise, considering starting one of your own, working with a team, or even on your own career, V-REEL is a tool you can use to aid and improve strategic thinking. It's a collection of the external and internal questions, considerations, and challenges that you will generally come across with any approach to strategy formulation. V-REEL gets at those ideas using simple language and straightforward tools to guide the thought process to sound conclusions that will leave you confident and with a clear path forward. So, whom will it help?

Entrepreneurs

If you are an entrepreneur, the V-REEL Framework will help you:

- Evaluate the rareness of resources and capabilities and form value propositions that will stand up to market conditions
- Articulate a clear, well-considered pitch that can stand up to investors' hard questions
- Form well-founded assumptions upon which to base financials
- Move forward with confidence that you've thought through considerations likely to impact your business

Executives

If you are an executive working in an existing business or corporate environment, V-REEL offers you and your team:

- A common framework and language that can be used within and across business units to aid productive discussion and inform decision making
- More informed, more justified, more reasoned discussion about go/no-go decisions
- A mechanism to help train up the next generation of corporate leaders and strategic thinkers

Product Managers

As a product manager, you're often under the gun to innovate while managing risk. V-REEL provides:

- A framework for evaluating market viability over time
- A proven tool to help you form clear product strategy
- Clarity regarding the key aspects of product plans

- Tools to help product managers anticipate and answer questions from the executive team

Not-for-Profit Executives

As an executive in the not-for-profit world, you need to deliver value as much as any organization but likely have fewer resources than your for-profit counterparts. V-REEL will help you:

- Discover how you create value in the market
- Identify how your value creation is, or could be, distinctive among other not-for-profits
- Understand what enabling resources you need to have in place to deliver promised value
- Think through how you might sustain your organization over time
- Establish a common language for use among team members and volunteers to foster effective communication

Individuals

As an individual who is thinking about how you can add value at work, in your career, in your community, and even at home, V-REEL is a framework that can help you:

- Think about and discover your personal, distinctive competencies
- Identify areas that are holding you back from being your most valuable
- Devise a plan for sharpening your distinctive competencies and developing new ones
- Think about how you will continue to be at your most valuable over time

What Will Readers Get Out of This book?

Ultimately, V-REEL is a framework to support decision making. As some wise person once said, the world is full of opportunities, and most of them are lousy. Put into practice, V-REEL will make it quite clear when a business or product idea is worth pursuing and when it is not. In this book, you will learn a process to identify which ideas to pursue and when to walk away. Spoiler alert—you should walk away from most.

But this isn't a pessimistic book, nor does V-REEL take a pessimistic perspective. On the contrary, what V-REEL offers is a mechanism for you and your team to REEL in your ideas and know with clarity which ones to throw back. In business and in life, we all need to have a realistic view, not a pessimistic view. Optimism comes from knowing that you've gone through a process, and you've thrown out the ideas that don't work for whatever reason. My hope is that you will use the V-REEL Framework to learn a new way to think beyond value about business operations, entrepreneurial endeavors, and personal objectives to gain a realistic view and define a plan for creating real competitive advantage in the market.

Once familiar with V-REEL, you will have at your disposal simple, straight-forward language to encourage strategic thinking and discussion among your team members. Together, you will be able to work through issues impacting rareness as well as eroding and enabling factors. You'll be able to consider all your planning in the context of time so that you can extend the life of your value creation and know when you need to be prepared with something new to offer the marketplace. As a framework for strategic thinking, V-REEL can help any leader think through and clearly communicate strategic issues and their root causes and identify solutions for exploiting or overcoming them.

How to Use This Book

In Chapter 1, I will provide a brief review of strategic management, defining key terms as well as common processes and tools that may be useful as you apply V-REEL to your situation. If strategic management is old hat to you, please skip the review and move on to what you find of value. Later in the chapter I'll introduce the V-REEL Framework, providing a look at the big picture before we jump into details.

Chapters 2–5 will take you through each aspect of the V-REEL Framework focusing on identifying and seeking to protect distinctive competencies. Each chapter will provide:

- The definition of the topic and how it relates to the other aspects of the framework
- Insight into why consideration of this aspect of your business is important
- An explanation of things to consider at this point of the framework
- A case study to place the topic in context of the real world
- Sample tools and tables to help you apply the topic to your own situation
- Suggested strategy tools and techniques you might use to support your strategy formulation

In Chapter 6, I will shift focus from value creation to an in-depth discussion of value destruction. We will walk through the entire V-REEL Framework in a second pass, this time in search of and resolving issues related to distinctive incompetencies.

Finally, Chapter 7 will provide specific recommendations for how to put V-REEL to work in your organization based on your particular role. I'll offer suggestions for the following:

- Executives in established businesses
- Entrepreneurs considering a new enterprise
- Not-for-profit organizations
- Individuals

In the back of the book you will find a glossary of terms so that you can quickly review topics as needed. V-REEL is designed to be simple and easy to apply such that it becomes a new, more complete way of thinking strategically. My hope is that this book will spur fresh thinking, encourage innovation and, very importantly, interject realism. If you step away from an idea because V-REEL helped you see its failings, I will count that as a success and hope you do too. And when V-REEL helps you to identify and overcome an eroding factor so that you can extend the life of your product or business model, I'll log that as a win as well. There is a lot of potential for wins here. If you realize that something isn't rare or can't be, that's a win. Simply being able to see some degree of prioritization so you know what you need to focus on first can be incredibly useful. If that's what you take from V-REEL, that's a win. Perhaps you find you are better able to name your distinctive competency or clearly realize a distinctive incompetency and how to get rid of it. Or maybe you'll identify an enabling factor that is missing or needs to be enhanced to realize a substantial increase in the longevity of your distinctive competency. There are lots of possibilities for wins. So let's get started. Let's think beyond value and get you and your team ready. We're accepting the challenge of the V-REEL Framework and we are going for the win.

CHAPTER 1

What to Know Before You Go

There's nothing worse than joining a conversation already in progress, hearing a familiar theme, and jumping in—only to realize you have no idea what you're talking about. You know you're in over your head. The group knows it and, if you're lucky, everyone awkwardly tries to move the conversation gracefully past your blunder. Best case, you're embarrassed, but the conversation moves ahead quickly. Worst case, misunderstanding leads to disagreement. Either way, a good conversation was interrupted because of a poor assumption. Most of us like to avoid making poor assumptions, and no one likes to be embarrassed. As we begin to think beyond value toward better strategy, let's avoid both of those situations with a quick review of strategic management. For those of you familiar with the discipline, the review will show how V-REEL works right along with many other approaches to strategy. For those less familiar, it will provide a foundation upon which we will build our framework throughout this book. Once we've reviewed strategic management, I will introduce the V-REEL Framework to provide a general sense of it before we dive into the details.

A Brief Review of Strategic Management

The big questions in strategic management are, why do some companies succeed and why do some fail, and what factors will determine the outcome? Historically, the strategic management discipline was developed by people who were economists, and they were looking at big manufacturing firms and focused on the external environment of businesses—those external events, conditions, entities, and other factors outside the organization that influence activities and impact opportunities and risk. Academics were looking to understand opportunities for efficiencies and economies of scale. Michael Porter, one of the founders of the modern strategy field and one of the world's most influential thinkers on management and competitiveness, took that industrial-organizational economic thinking, reworked it, and put it into management literature as his Five Forces Analysis. Porter's model aids business strategy development by providing a mechanism for understanding and analyzing the level of competition within an industry. The following are of concern, according to Porter's Five Forces:

- The threat of substitute products or services
- The threat of established rivals
- The threat of new entrants
- The bargaining power of suppliers
- The bargaining power of customers

From there, Porter turned his focus to the internal environment. He developed the value-chain concept which looks at the processes within an organization with the understanding that how those activities are carried out determines costs and impacts profits. By the late 1980s, others had joined Porter in thinking and writing about the need to focus on what was happening inside the organization. There was a growing awareness that, while the external environment was important, it was not the whole story by any means. Not enough attention had been paid to what was going on inside organizations.

 The big questions are, why do some companies succeed and why do some fail, and what factors will determine the outcome?

The resource-based view (RBV) of the firm, first widely presented in 1984 in a *Strategic Management Journal* article by Birger Wernerfelt, takes the position that it is the unique qualities inside an organization that play the larger role in its success. From research conducted in the decades since then, we know that success results from a mix of internal and external factors. Roughly 20 percent of success is attributable to external factors unique to the industry in which it participates, and about 36 percent to internal factors.[8] The remaining balance includes things that we either do not understand or cannot measure well, such as luck, personal relationships, and trust. The resource-based view, while presumably focused on the internal environment, boils down to a series of questions that you should ask yourself about your organization. In reality, you must do all the thinking about the external environment to answer those internally focused questions.

The first resource-based view question is simple but powerful: What are your key resources and capabilities that are creating value for you? Keep in mind, when we're talking about value, you must understand that value is measured in the ability to create more value than you consume. You consume value to create value—think inputs vs. outputs. So, you're looking for the things inside your organization that make that incremental change in value. With that in mind, we ask the question, what are the key resources and capabilities inside your organization that create value?

Resources can be tangible or intangible. Your tangible resources are your plant, your equipment, your supplies, your people—those physical, tangible assets. But many of your resources are going to be intangible—things like imagination, creativity, skills, knowledge, reputation, and trust—all the soft and intangible things that are real and incredibly important, but you can't touch, smell, or see. You take these resources—both tangible and intangible—and you use them to develop capabilities. Capabilities are the essential implementations of your resources—the capability to do web design, develop branding narratives, offer great service, make an awesome pizza, etc. You're hoping to identify the resource base that you have and then zero in on your key value creating resources and capabilities.

After you do that, you ask the next question: Are any of these key resources and capabilities rare? You ask because it's great that you've got something that can create value, but if everybody else has it too, then as soon as you bring that value into the marketplace, competitors will recognize the value there, and they will enter the market employing their similar resources and capabilities. You won't be able to make any real margin. You won't be able to win in the market because there isn't anything to set you apart from the competition. You want some degree of rareness.

The next question then follows: How do you create rareness? Some of the things that we talk about regarding Porter's Five Forces and barriers to entry could create rareness for you by keeping others from being able to do what you're doing. Or maybe you can create literal rareness in the sense that you are truly the only one that has a particular capability in your market. Some human skills, like reputation and trust, can often be very difficult for others to replicate, and so those intangible factors can be rare and very valuable. You hope for some degree of rareness. And then you hope for some degree of inimitability and non-substitutability. You don't want people to be able to figure out how to imitate your value proposition or substitute something else for the value that you're creating.

In the strategy world, people often remember considerations of the resource-based view of the firm with the letters *VRIS* (Value, Rareness, Inimitability, non-Substitutability). The idea of the resource-based view of the firm is to run your ideas through the VRIS filter, and if you have or can create value, rareness, and a high difficulty of imitation *and* substitution, then there is a good chance you have something workable. You might recall the first two considerations of V-REEL and note the familiar theme—V: Value, R: Rareness. I'll present both value and rareness in detail later, but I want to point out how V-REEL captures the themes of existing and proven strategy methods.

If you discover that you have some key resources that are value creating, are rare, hard to imitate, and hard to substitute, then you may have a distinctive competency in the marketplace. Some people refer to these as core competencies, but I like to think of core competencies as those things that you do exceptionally well in your organization. But the ones that make it through the VRIS filter with flying colors— those are your distinctive competencies. They are distinctive because they set you apart in the marketplace in terms of the ability to create value. Some people may refer to core competencies and talk about them the way I talk about distinctive competencies, but I like to clarify the difference between those two terms. On the one hand, you have core competencies—things that you do particularly well to create value. These may be very important things, perhaps even critical enablers which we will get to later, but the resources and capabilities that make it through the VRIS screen or are much closer to making it through that screen are your real distinctive competencies. When you work through the V-REEL Framework, those distinctive competencies will become the primary focus of your strategic thinking.

 When you have a competitive advantage, you've created value for which people will pay a premium; that competitive advantage is driven by the distinctiveness of your competencies.

As you're developing a business or product concept, you hope to have some distinctive competencies. You also hope that the combination of those distinctive competencies will lead you to a true competitive advantage in the marketplace. And by that, I mean you can make real profits because you have market power, you can charge considerably above input costs, win the market competition, and have a true competitive advantage in the marketplace. A true competitive advantage means I am outperforming my competitors; I have better returns than my competitors, and thus, I have more to reinvest in my business in such things as advertising and marketing. That investment then propels me even further ahead of competitors. When you have a competitive advantage, you've created value for which people will pay a premium; that competitive advantage is driven by the *distinctiveness* of your competencies.

To identify distinctive competencies, you need to understand your external environment because many of the answers to questions in the VRIS filter come from that understanding. For instance— what's valuable? To answer that question, you must know what your customers—your buyers—are willing to buy. You must understand the demographic influences, the macroeconomic influences, all the other general environmental influences, the industry forces of your rivals, etc., to be able to answer this question: In what are people finding value? And of course, that's subjective. Whatever customers are willing to pay for is valuable.

In terms of answering what's rare, what's hard to imitate, and what's hard to substitute, you must know the external environment because you've got to know your competitors, your industry conditions, and how they affect the market. You still must understand your external environment to answer those questions. But during this time of searching for distinctive competencies, you are focusing very much internally and going through an introspective analysis of who you are as an organization and what you're doing in the context of the external environment. We will use the V-REEL Framework to think beyond value creation and bridge that gap between the internal and external environments. We want to look at both internal and external issues simultaneously and think our way to a clear path forward. Before we do that, let's talk about a few strategy methods and tools that might be useful along the way.

The V-REEL Approach to Strategy

The concepts of distinctive competencies and distinctive incompetencies are central to the usefulness of V-REEL for strategy formulation. It is these opportunities and challenges that the framework helps you to identify and address, helping you move closer to achieving a sustained competitive advantage in the marketplace. Given how important competencies and incompetencies are, let's begin our introduction to V-REEL with a clear definition of each.

Distinctive Competencies

Foods with a distinctive flavor are easy to identify. Horseradish is spicy and powerful. Strawberries are sweet. Even if you don't necessarily care for them, you would probably never say they taste like chicken. Meriam-Webster offers a simple definition of distinctive: "Appealing or interesting because of an unusual quality or characteristic." Unusual is a great word. It conjures the idea of rareness. Distinctive competencies aren't simply things that your company can do well. Doing something well, in and of itself, is never a guarantee of true value creation—the kind that enables you to generate more value than is required to deliver in the marketplace. When I talk about distinctive competencies, I am referring to those underlying resources and capabilities—either tangible or intangible—that can create value in the marketplace *and* that are rare. Sometimes business owners overlook what they have that is distinctive. They fail to recognize the real resource or capability that sets them apart in the marketplace.

For instance, I'm sure Coca-Cola is very aware that it has marketing and distribution capabilities that enable it to make water—an extremely ordinary, and therefore not-rare resource in the developed world—something special and valuable. The water itself is not the distinctive competency. In the case of Dasani Water, the distinctive competencies are related to distribution channels and brand loyalty. But suppose you're talking to a local restaurant owner. That owner could be convinced that it is his family recipes that make all the difference and set him apart in his market. He might argue that the secret family recipe is the distinctive competency that keeps people coming back for more. But if the business is doing well, it could very well be the elements of trust, familiarity, and friendliness that distinguish his restaurant experience from others.

People like the owner or like the feel of the place—the experience. They can get that same dish or something very similar somewhere else, but they choose to keep going to the local pizza place because the employees are nice, and they make the customers feel like family.

Very often there are intangibles working alongside other tangible resources. Business owners often fail to realize that it is actually the intangibles that set them apart and are the real distinctive competencies. In both cases—water and pizza—we are dealing with products that are not especially rare, but in both cases, there is a resource or capability behind the product that combines with the product to create value, and not just value, but also rareness. When you have that combination, then you have a distinctive competency. And that is what needs to be protected from erosion and supported with enabling resources and capabilities. We'll cover more on that later.

Distinctive Incompetencies

We've established that distinctiveness is associated with this idea of rareness that is so important to value creation. But when we are talking about distinctive incompetencies we are concerned with value destruction or things that might destroy your ability to create value. While a distinctive competency's degree of rareness increases its value, the rareness of a distinctive *in*competency could actually increase its potentially negative impact on your ability to create value. Returning to the pizza restaurant example, imagine all the brands of pizza delivery places you know. Now imagine that one of those places has horrible customer service—orders are wrong, employees are inattentive and rude, and deliveries are late. With all other things being equal or basically the same—and most chain pizzas are about the same—you're going to avoid the one with horrible customer service. So that distinctive incompetency—poor customer service that makes one pizza company different from all the others—is rare in the market to the degree that customers can choose a comparable offering and avoid bad customer service. Poor customer service destroyed the ability for that pizza place to deliver value in the marketplace. You can imagine how that could be devastating to a business. We will use V-REEL to identify distinctive incompetencies and determine what needs to be done to remove or diminish their impact on your ability to deliver value.

The V-REEL Framework

As we begin to move through the V-REEL Framework, we will first focus on identifying and working with distinctive competencies that fuel value creation. Once we've done that, we will turn our focus to distinctive incompetencies and learn to identify those places where you are actually destroying your ability to create value. From there, we can determine how to address any issues of incompetence. But first, let's get oriented to the V-REEL Framework. The diagram in Figure 1: The V-REEL Framework provides an overview so you can begin to visualize how it can be used to REEL in ideas and improve processes toward a more strategic operation.

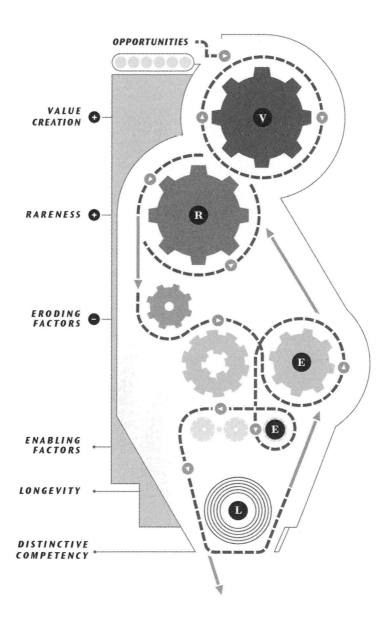

Figure 1: The V-REEL Framework

Value and Rareness

By now you know that the *V* and the *R* in V-REEL are value and rareness. In considering these two aspects of your business, you'll need to ask the very same questions that you ask regarding the resource-based view of the firm:

- How are you creating value?
- What resources and capabilities are behind that value creation?
- Are they rare?

When thinking about value, I ask if I have something customers will buy that will create value for them. Then I try to identify the key resources and capabilities that create the competencies underlying that value—always keeping in mind that the source of competencies could be either tangible or intangible. Having completed the resource inventory and identified key resources and capabilities, I then need to ask, are any of my resources and capabilities rare at all, and if so, why? What makes them rare?

Triseum is a start-up educational gaming company that is setting out to change higher education with video games. The company intends to insert commercial-grade video games into academic programs right alongside textbooks to make it fun to learn hard subjects like calculus. Neat idea, right? But what makes Triseum rare? There are quite a few gaming companies out there. Might they also be able to bring games to academia? Triseum, though, has something unique. The company is aligned with a major university that is known for its animation and visualization program and has an on-campus laboratory where games can be tested for educational efficacy. How many other gaming companies have such a relationship that brings very valuable resources like a testing lab complete with student users? Not too many. That's rare. So, in the case of Triseum, one of the distinctive competencies is the relationship between the company and the university.

 Things start to get interesting when you determine that you have something that is both valuable and rare in the marketplace.

As you'll see throughout this book, relationships are often the very things that set companies apart in the marketplace and enable them to deliver value. As an entrepreneur or executive, it is important when developing strategy to understand what those key resources and capabilities are underneath your competencies that enable you to create value. Then you need to understand *if* those resources and capabilities are rare and *why* they are rare. This will tell you what to protect and what might need to be developed around those resources and capabilities to create some rareness.

The rareness discussion can help you think about how you're creating value, and it can help you see if you need to add something to create value that is also rare. It all rolls up together. These are not clean, distinctive steps that allow you to stop thinking about value once you've moved on to rareness. You keep circling back and refining. When—if—you come up with something that is both valuable and rare, then you have a potential distinctive competency. And with that potential in place, things start to get interesting. Keep in mind that while the presence of distinctive competencies is necessary for business success, it is not sufficient. We must now move on to V-REEL's first *E*—Eroding Factors.

Eroding Factors

Given what you know about both your external and internal environments, what is going to work against you over time to erode your ability to create value or your ability to have rareness? Here we are specifically focused on those distinctive competencies identified in the value and rareness discussion. We are not going to concern ourselves with anything else at this point because the resources and capabilities that form your distinctive competencies are the heart of your business. These are the resources and the capabilities that enable you to create value through your competencies, and thus, they all need to be protected from eroding factors. Say you've gone through your thinking of value and rareness and realized that your key resource is the creative ability of one specific person on your team. What if that person leaves or gets hit by the proverbial bus? That is an example of an eroding factor. I will talk more about different types of eroding factors in Chapter 3.

For now, just keep in mind we are thinking about eroding factors that could chip away at distinctive competencies or destroy them all together. But we need to be efficient and think about eroding factors in a prioritized way. After all, some things are far more likely to occur than others. Similarly, if some things were to occur, they would be more devastating than others. With V-REEL, we've created a matrix that you can use to rate what is most likely to occur and how big the impact might be on your ability to create value or be rare in the marketplace. We will go into the Erosion Matrix in more detail later. For now, it is simply important to understand that the matrix will help you identify those eroding factors that present the greatest threat to your ability to create value. Knowing what your distinctive competencies are and understanding where erosion of rareness presents potential issues, you can begin to think about the second *E*—Enabling Factors.

Enabling Factors

By the time you get to enabling factors, if you really understand your key resources and capabilities and have thought through the eroding factors, then you're probably beginning to get a good idea of where you need to pay attention. The Erosion Matrix has helped you to prioritize and focus your strategic thinking. With fresh understanding of your distinctive competencies, their rareness, and any factors that may erode that rareness, you're ready to consider your other resources and capabilities: the ones that don't quite make it to the level of distinctive competencies but might be key to erosion control. The idea here is to use enabling resources to protect and extend the life of your value creation. These key resources and capabilities are the second *E* of V-REEL, and we call them enabling factors. Like many of the items in Porter's Value Chain map, they may be very supportive in nature, such as accounting systems, human resources, delivery partners, and other functions that make the organizational system work. Or they could be necessary only to blunt the impact of an eroding factor. For instance, if a business operation relies on certain government regulations, the company may need to have the capability to lobby the government to help ensure things do not change. The ability to lobby effectively and remain aware of the political situation becomes a key enabling factor for the business.

It is important to have the enabling resources and capabilities to blunt eroding factors and to support the ongoing creation of value. Too often, entrepreneurs will get caught up in the aspects of value delivery that they know, but they'll neglect to give necessary attention to factors that enable them to do the thing they love. We all want to do the thing we love—I get that. If you want to spend the least amount of time possible on what might be the less enjoyable aspects of the business, you once again need to prioritize and focus. Some enabling factors may be far more important than others. If you have an eroding factor with potentially huge impact sitting out there, you may need to develop an enabling factor like that lobbying capability. And rather than worry about it later, you may need to put that enabling factor in place soon because that eroding factor could absolutely destroy your ability to create value.

You don't want to waste time and resources on things unlikely to impact your value creation, but do invest time developing the enabling factors you really must have in place to protect value and rareness. And in thinking through both eroding and enabling factors, you need to be thinking about *time* so you have some sense of how long it will be before things change and eroding factors become a problem. You need to know when change might occur. You also need to know when you would need additional resources. You invest the time in that kind of dynamic thinking so you can extend the life of your value proposition. Which brings us to the *L* in V-REEL—Longevity.

Longevity

In all the considerations thus far, we've really been taking a snapshot of the world today and understanding how things are currently set. But as the old saying goes, time doesn't stand still for anyone. We all should at least try to guess when eroding factors might occur and when we might need enabling factors to kick in. We need to give our best estimate of how long this snapshot of the world today will hold. How long before my potential for competitive advantage disappears or changes? If I have a pretty good handle on when eroding factors can occur and when enabling factors can be put into place, I might have a pretty decent estimation of how long I have to enjoy a potential competitive advantage in the marketplace. And because you've done all the work leading up to this point, by now you can usually start to see where you can adjust your operation to extend that time and push erosion down the road. By the time we come to discussion of longevity, you can really see what needs to be addressed right away and what other things can be addressed a little bit later.

Apple provides a great view of how considerations of longevity come into play over the life of a company and product. When the company first introduced the iPhone after many years of research and development, I imagine Apple had planned that its competitive advantage was going to hold for so many months before competitors entered the market. And it did. There was a transition period when the competitors were coming into the market but their products were inferior. By 2016, Apple had lost some of that competitive advantage because the competitors' products were very capable substitutes. But Apple knew this would be the case, so it invested significantly to build up a very powerful intangible—the Apple brand. Through exceptional branding and marketing, Apple has positioned itself as the best, the coolest, and the obvious choice if you can afford it. Apple has done such a great job building its brand that customers are willing to pay a premium for the product largely because of the brand image. The Apple brand, together with other key enabling factors such as supply chain optimization and supplier relationships, supports the strength of the company's value and rareness, and has extended the life of Apple's competitive advantage in the cell phone market.

Even so, Apple continues to look to the future. Leadership knows that cell phones are rapidly becoming commodities, and like every other company, Apple must look to the future, figure out how long it can expect to enjoy the status quo, and then be ready with the next big thing when the situation changes. No matter the size of your business or popularity of your brand, your competitive advantage has a shelf life. Using the V-REEL Framework to identify your distinctive competencies and build a strategy to defend, extend, and even prepare to replace them can significantly improve your ability to create value and even achieve sustainable competitive advantage.

Considering Incompetencies

Value creation is the goal, and thus the focus of strategy formulation tools and processes, but most tools miss a major source of potential value creation: removing value destruction. It is useful to go back through the V-REEL Framework, this time looking for distinctive incompetencies. You must ask:

- Where am I destroying value?
- Where am I doing things that might reduce the value of something, and what are the resources and capabilities that are causing the problem?
- Is this problem common in my marketplace or is this something that is unique to my company?
- Do we have any distinctive incompetencies because of these resources and capabilities?

You must next consider what the eroding factors are that would fix the problem. Instead of eroding away the value and the rareness, what are the eroding factors that would increase your ability to create value and at least bring you to parity with the competition and make your incompetency not rare? Remember, when you are talking about distinctive incompetencies, rareness is bad—think about the only pizza place with terrible customer service—so eroding away the rare incompetency is a really good thing! You are looking for enabling factors that are necessary to put into place to make sure erosion happens. So, what resources and capabilities can you enable in your organization to overcome the incompetencies? And then, when considering longevity, ask yourself how long the incompetency will last and how you can shorten that timeframe. Do you need to fire someone? Add training to the mix? Perhaps you need a whole new competency. The key to this part of your strategic thinking is to look honestly at your resources and capabilities. It's not the most popular aspect of your planning efforts, but it is essential to your ability to compete and win in your market.

 You can't just create distinctive competencies and you can't just eliminate distinctive incompetencies. You must do both to achieve a competitive advantage.

In the first pass through V-REEL, you're looking for distinctive competencies and what's going to erode them away; you then build up defenses against erosion and preserve your competencies for as long as possible. In the second pass through V-REEL, you're hunting down incompetencies and you're trying to figure out how to get rid of them. The interesting thing about this—from a strategic standpoint—is that you really need to complete both passes. You can't *just* create distinctive competencies and you can't *just* eliminate distinctive incompetencies. You must do both to achieve a competitive advantage. Why? Because you could be creating great distinctive competencies but have massive distinctive *in*competencies that offset all the value creation. As a result, you don't really have a competitive advantage at all. It's like trying to drive the car forward with one foot on the brake. You go nowhere. Similarly, you can spend all your time trying to eliminate the distinctive incompetencies but never create distinctive competencies, and the best you can hope for is parity with everybody else. You must be working on both. You should be working simultaneously to identify incompetencies—making sure you don't have any that are holding you back—while you are hunting down the ability to have distinctive competencies that will set you apart and give you a competitive advantage. It's a lot of work. But it is also quite rewarding. Using the V-REEL Framework as your guide, you can proceed with your strategy formulation knowing that the effort will be worthwhile. So let's begin. We will start our journey through the V-REEL Framework searching for value and rareness as we gain new insights into the external and internal environments. There is much to learn, but this is the way to the win.

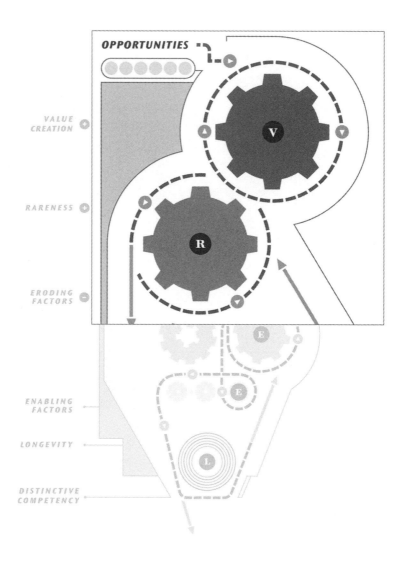

OPPORTUNITIES

VALUE
CREATION

RARENESS

ERODING
FACTORS

ENABLING
FACTORS

LONGEVITY

DISTINCTIVE
COMPETENCY

V

R

E

E

L

CHAPTER 2

The Quest: Seeking Value and Rareness

L ike Columbus sailing off to find a route to India, Ponce de Leon searching for the fabled fountain of youth, or Indiana Jones seeking the Ark of the Covenant, there are grand quests in our lives and in our imaginations. You may not know it yet, but you are pursuing a grand quest. Your quest is to create value and have that value be rare. But sometimes you find something different from what you expected, or you are searching for something that doesn't exist. And sometimes you find something better and far more powerful than you ever imagined. One thing is certain, if you do not set out on a quest to create value and rareness, others will—and you will be left behind.

Consider Johnny. He really loves history, so he set out to pursue a degree in history from a reputable university. He was willing to make that investment because he values history, and his time in college was great. Johnny genuinely enjoyed his studies, he was active in history clubs, and he even ventured to historic sites to really dig into the topic. But as graduation approached, he began job hunting and was really disappointed to learn that the study of history that he so valued did not seem to be much in demand among employers. He saw lots of jobs posted for people with engineering degrees and business degrees, but there wasn't even a career fair for history majors. Johnny is about to be left behind. What happened?

Johnny failed to realize that he doesn't get to define value in the employment marketplace; the employers do. While there are employers who value people with history degrees, it seems that there is some additional value-added capability needed to make a history degree truly valuable to most employers. The same is true for any business. The market defines what is valuable, and that's why this idea of value is one that is most talked about in existing business strategy processes. Most often you hear value talked about in terms of a value proposition, an innovative product, service, or feature that will make your product or company attractive to customers. Popular books and tools like the *Business Model Canvas* aim to help businesses leaders think about and hone their value propositions so they can avoid Johnny's mistake—so they are sure to think through their value creation from the market's perspective. That's important, but before we go any further into this discussion of value, I want to distinguish quickly between value propositions and what you need to be thinking about when I am talking about the *V* in V-REEL. You do need to have an idea of your value proposition—or what you think it might be. But here we are thinking beyond the value proposition. We are going deeper, if you will, to understand the resources and capabilities that form that value. We do so because as a business owner, executive, entrepreneur, or working individual, you are seeking a competitive position in your market, and it is not enough to have a value proposition. You must also understand what key resources and capabilities enable you to deliver that value so you can use your strategy-formulation time wisely and build up and protect the resources and capabilities that matter most. In this chapter I will focus on value, the resources and capabilities that enable you to create value, and that essential element called rareness that is central to any discussion of value creation.

Resources and Capabilities Inventory

We begin our journey through the V-REEL Framework with an idea; call it a draft of your value proposition. It is an expression of how you believe you will create value in your marketplace, whether that market is other businesses, a consumer market, a service sector, or, if you are an individual seeking employment, the workforce. In all cases, you need to create value, and to begin you must have some sense of how you are going to create that value. To do that, you need to think about what you want to do and the resources and capabilities that might enable you to do it. You must articulate your value proposition and then enumerate the resources and capabilities required to deliver that value proposition. And that's kind of a loop. You start out thinking what you might like to do and then about resources and capabilities and what you can do, or even perhaps what you could do given some additional resources. This should lead you to thinking about your market, because to create value in a market you must offer something that is both sought after and, to some extent, rare. You'll naturally talk about how you can create value by doing this or that. In a typical strategic-planning meeting the group might be asking about the new product initiative, the new theme for the year, the company's new vision, or things along those lines. The initial goal is to articulate how you might create value and then create an initial inventory of the resources and capabilities you think are required to create and deliver that value.

Defining Value

What do I mean by value? This may seem obvious, but let's spend just a few minutes here making sure we are talking about the same thing. Because everyone understands what it is to value something, right? But try to define value in the context of your business, organization, or even your professional value and it can start to get a bit tricky. Let me try to simplify it: value is a perception inside a person's head such that if that person says something is valuable, it is. A measure of that value is the amount of money the person is willing to exchange for the thing, service, or experience. It's really that simple. Economists have lots of terms they use to define value and many measures for value, but ultimately it comes down to the consumer's perception of a product, service, or experience. This is very important to understand for two reasons: One, so you can get to know your consumers and understand what they value. And two, so you can recognize that *you are not your consumer*. You do not define what is valuable in the marketplace. Your consumer defines what is valuable and, therefore, *understanding your consumer* is the first key to understanding how you might be able to create value.

Remember Johnny? He really loves history but found out the hard way that a history degree alone wasn't quite enough to create real value in the marketplace and land a job that pays enough to justify the investment in the history degree. Now consider Johnny's roommate, Joseph. Joseph is also a history major, but instead of traveling to historical sites, Joseph decided to take a few extra hours and get a teaching certificate. He also did an unpaid internship with the local history museum where he built a summer program that used theater to teach kids about history. When Joseph was ready to look for jobs, he had some additional value to add to his history degree. He knew he might not make as much money as his engineering and business school buddies, but he is happy—prepared with a strong résumé—to apply for teaching jobs where he will have the opportunity to share his love of history.

The difference between Johnny and Joseph is simple. Joseph recognized who his consumer was going to be when it was time to find a job after college. He took steps to ensure that he would be of value to that consumer when the time came to apply for jobs. Johnny, on the other hand, made an all-too-common mistake. He assumed that because he valued history, his future employers would as well.

 You are not your consumer. You do not define what is valuable in the marketplace. Your consumer does.

Maybe this seems like a really simple example, but don't let its simplicity fool you. Entrepreneurs and even established businesses behave like Johnny all the time. They get so wrapped up in what they love doing (or are excited about) that they forget to consider if they are actually able to deliver something the consumer will value. Back in 1993, Apple introduced the Newton MessagePad. One of the first handheld devices to offer basic computing, the Newton was touted to offer handwriting recognition. While initial enthusiasm was high—after all this was technology way ahead of its time—the engineers were not able to get the handwriting recognition capability working right for the initial release. As a result, the Newton was a flop, and critics mocked the device as a $700 alternative to a perfectly effective paper pad and pen. What killed the Apple Newton? Inability to deliver on a big idea and a market that wasn't quite ready to give up paper.

Checking in with the consumer, understanding your market, and having a realistic understanding of your resources and capabilities are all critical to understanding your potential for creating value. Value creation depends on far more than simple demand. There might be great demand for something that you can create or offer to the market; however, if you are not able to provide that value in such a way that it creates more value than is required to deliver it, then you're not actually creating value at all. You're not actually able to earn a profit. Remember, profit is the difference between the value you create and the value you consume.

So how do you create more value than you consume? There are many factors that contribute to your potential to create value—both inside and outside your organization. We can gain great insight into these factors and learn about value creation and potential for rareness in the market through external and internal analyses. But don't be fooled. This is not simple number crunching that might be delegated to a machine. This is a hunt. Your awareness should be heightened. Your senses peaked. We are on a hunt for value, but not just any value—value that is rare.

In Search of Distinctive Competencies

So here you are, ready to hunt. Armed with an idea and enthusiasm, you are pretty sure you understand how you might create value, and you have some sense of what's required to bring that idea to market. You're *pretty* sure. That's great! At this point, "pretty sure" is awesome because if you know you're only pretty sure, that means you're open to learning what the market has to teach you. And that is the key to unlocking that treasure chest of value. You must remain open and teachable, willing to accept the lessons this hunt can offer. You must even be willing to turn back. After all, we are in search of distinctive competencies which, by definition, are both valuable and rare. It is quite likely you will discover that you do not, in fact, have the resources and capabilities to deliver value. Or you might find out that the market doesn't value that thing you think so grand. That's okay. That is a great thing to know at this point. Imagine if Coca-Cola had taken the time to understand its consumers better before spending millions to launch New Coke. I mean really, are any of us who are outside of Coca-Cola at all surprised that didn't work? Coke is Coke. It can't be *new*. It's classic! But that is easier for us to see because we are outside of Coca-Cola, not blinded by the fear of declining market share and profits. So go ahead. Get outside of your own ideas and take some time to explore the external environment. It has a lot to teach you.

Exploring the External Environment

At this point in the V-REEL Framework, we are considering value and rareness in an effort to find and understand your distinctive competencies. You are looking at the resources and capabilities identified during your initial inventory and asking the following questions:

- Which of these is key to creating value?
- Are any of these rare?
- Can I create rareness from or around any of them?

If you are the only person in the world who has a specific resource or a unique capability that someone values, then obviously you are in a better position than others to create value. They can't do what you can do. Or they don't have what you have. The only way to determine if what you have is valuable or rare is to look outside yourself or your organization and seek to understand the external environment and your consumers. Following is a brief introduction to the things about which you need to be thinking and trying to understand as you're getting acquainted with your external environment. To simplify your external analysis, I created Figure 2: Exploring the External Environment. This simple figure combines considerations from Porter's Five Forces Analysis, as well as market and non-market forces into a single image to help you visualize and recall the various aspects to consider during your external analysis. You need to consider if and how any of these things might affect your potential value creation. As you do, you'll begin to see how you stand up in the market. I'll begin with a look at market and non-market factors: those market conditions that are directly and immediately related to your specific business activities in your industry, and those general, more distant non-market factors that could still impact your organization in indirect ways. The reality is the market and non-market factors are intertwined and should be considered together. Let's spend a bit of time getting familiar with a few of the more important market and general non-market factors that you need to consider.

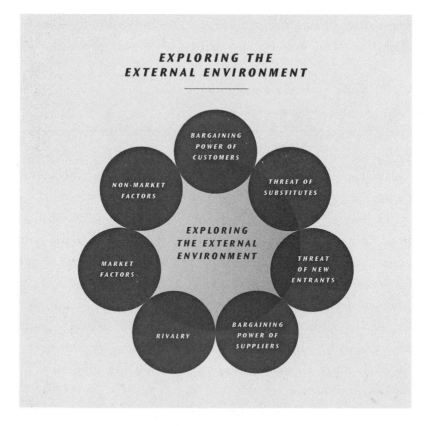

Figure 2: Exploring the External Environment

Market Factors

Market factors that you handle on an almost daily basis are likely to be easy for you to imagine and consider because they are close to and related to your operation. Some typical market factors to consider include:

- The available workforce
- Demographic characteristics of your customers in the target market
- The cost of your supplies, office space, and equipment
- Availability of capital and banking services
- The competing products or services from existing competitors

These market factors and others probably come to mind very naturally as you're planning your operations, but there is another force often at work in markets that you need to consider—complements. Complementary products and services can be a powerful driver of sales. Think of peanut butter. Now what do you almost always need to have with it? Jelly, of course. These are complements. The sale of one very likely impacts the sale of the other. Car insurance is a complement to a vehicle purchase, so much so that people often select a car to minimize the cost of insurance. Services benefit from complements as well. Think of the optometrists located in shopping malls and Walmart stores. Perhaps this relationship isn't quite so tight as peanut butter to jelly, but it is still a complement because people regularly visit the mall and Walmart. By locating where people are going to be, the optometrist is better positioned to get business. Likewise, pharmacies open locations in big-box stores, such as Target, in hopes of capturing additional customers. As you're thinking about your value and rareness, consider what is going on around you that might present opportunities for distinctiveness. Complements are often a good source.

Non-Market Factors

Non-market factors are more general and less obvious than market factors, and as a result, organizations often will overlook these aspects of the external environment. But non-market factors can significantly affect your ability to create value and should not be ignored. Things like politics, the economy, sociocultural trends, or changes in technology are important to think about as you get to know your external environment.

Politics, Media, and Activism

Politics are powerful, both globally and locally. While political factors are generally out of an organization's realm of control, lobbying, public relations, contributions, and even litigation are among the tools organizations employ to influence political decisions in their favor. The regulatory environment within any given industry may be highly influenced by special interest groups because regulations can have significant effects on operations and the resulting potential for profits. No matter your business, it's a good idea to stay tuned in to the political issues in your industry and local community. You may need to become active in the process to protect your organization's interests. Plus, politics are often deeply intertwined with media coverage of issues and activism from interest groups. All three tend to influence and amplify each other. Staying on top of what is happening around you in the mix of news, activism, and politics may, at the very least, provide some prior notice about what challenges your business will confront or opportunities to pursue.

Macro-Economic Factors

Economic factors, such as employment rates, interest rates, and growth trends, while clearly falling outside the realm of control of any given organization, have significant effects on our ability to create value. When unemployment is high, you may offer lower salaries to new hires and could invest savings into training and development. On the other hand, if the supply of highly skilled labor is limited, you're probably going to be compelled to pay a premium for that workforce, meaning you'll have to pass those costs on to customers or suffer lower profit. The cost of capital is, of course, highly influenced by interest rates which are also influenced by the political environment. You can begin to see how these factors all intertwine to shape the external environment and why it is so important to stay aware.

Sociocultural and Demographic Trends

Social trends, demographic changes, and cultural influences have huge effects on whole industries. Sometimes trends are lasting, but other times there are limited windows of opportunity to take advantage of trends in the marketplace. Social and cultural pressures to be more environmentally responsible have affected everything from the automotive industry to food production and much more. Changes in fashion trends drive the clothing industry, while increased cultural awareness has spurred the rise of social entrepreneurship with whole new models for developing and funding businesses that purport to address social, cultural, and environmental issues. The movement of the Millennial generation into the workforce will reshape demand for many industries such as housing, education, and transportation. That generation has begun to exhibit different preferences and priorities as compared to prior generations. Of course, trends differ across markets, so you must know to whom you're selling and what they value to deliver value in a way that fits with the current sociocultural and demographic setting. The key word there is *current*. Things are always, always changing. You've got to remain vigilant as you continually scan the marketplace.

Technology

Changes in technology over the last twenty years have dramatically influenced virtually every other aspect of the external environment. Ubiquitous personal computing and internet access across the developed world combined with mobile computing to raise consumer awareness of sociocultural, environmental, economic, and political issues. Of course, technology also affords opportunities for enhanced efficiencies in manufacturing and logistics. Meanwhile, thanks to advances in mobile computing, disruptive new business models have emerged in the sharing economy made so prominent by the likes of Uber and AirBNB. And of course, nothing changes faster than technology, so you can't afford to look away long. Who knows what opportunities might emerge with the next big thing in tech?

Ecology

Organizations operate in the natural environment, regardless of where they might be located. It has always been the case, and certainly is not less so today, that organizations benefit when they pay attention to and protect the environment in which they operate and upon which they often depend. Farmers have long understood the need to conserve soil if they want to maximize crop yields. And due to both sociocultural and political changes, mining and forestry operations along with other natural resource-based industries are now held accountable for environmental damage mitigation. The use of recyclable supplies and recycling practices can lend credibility to a brand in some consumer markets. And of course, man-made environmental disasters that make headlines can be devastating to an organization's public image. Also, any business operating in an area where nature can disrupt the market with a hurricane, earthquake, or other natural disaster must consider that risk. It's a good idea to take the time to understand what ecological issues might directly or indirectly benefit or potentially harm your ability to create value.

Legal Factors

The legal environment in which you operate is comprised of all the relevant rules, regulations, and laws within which you must abide. Naturally, these can have a significant effect on how, when, and where you do business, and as such, may very likely change your ability to create value. From an international perspective, import/export laws can either open or limit supplier options, thus influencing costs. Locally, things like zoning laws and development regulations may be advantageous or could add to the cost of setting up shop. Here's the bottom line: you need to know your legal environment and determine if you can create value while playing by the rules.

Also, please keep in mind that many of these non-market factors which might influence your ability to create value are now globalized in their effects. Political and legal issues are different every time your business or operation crosses a border. The sociocultural trends that arose in China have influenced the production of entertainment in Hollywood. Movies with big production budgets, like the superhero movies that have become so popular, often are made with the Chinese market in mind in hopes of capturing that customer base. You must question the market and non-market forces happening outside of your home market in our big, interconnected world. Those forces just might change the way you think about how to create value and discover rareness. Keeping a global perspective may become a crucial part of finding your distinctive competencies.

Now we come to the traditional five industry forces that were popularized by Michael Porter decades ago. The forces overlap with some of what we've already seen in the external environment, but because these five forces are so widely known and referred to in strategy circles, I'll briefly discuss them.

Threat of New Entrants

Do you remember when there was only one frozen yogurt shop in your town? For about six months, that yogurt shop had long lines (or at least a steady flow of customers). But before long, a slew of other frozen yogurt shops opened all over town. Entrepreneurs saw the popularity of frozen yogurt and ease of entry into the business, and virtually overnight there appeared a frozen yogurt shop seemingly at every corner. Each new yogurt shop chipped away at the rareness of existing shops. And both the existing and new entrants in the local frozen yogurt market had to work that much harder to compete for customers. Ultimately, not all the yogurt businesses survived because there simply was not enough demand in the market to support many frozen yogurt shops.

Just like those yogurt shops, when new entrants join any market, consumers enjoy more options. That, in turn, can prompt existing organizations to lower their prices to remain competitive or spend more on products and services to differentiate themselves. In both cases, the net effect is decreased profitability. Here is the bottom line: when new entrants appear in the market, they change the rules of the game. So, when considering your potential for creating value in a given market, it's important to ask this question: How easy might it be for *others* to enter the market and chip away at *my* competitiveness?

Bargaining Power of Suppliers and Buyers

The fewer supplier options available for buyers of a given product or service, the greater the power those suppliers exert in the market. Highly specialized materials or manufactured products might result in a strong supplier bargaining position simply because there are few sources of their products or services. They are rare. On the other side of the same coin, buyers enjoy strong bargaining power when there is little differentiation among product offerings. I mention bargaining power of suppliers and bargaining power of buyers separately to be sure you consider both. When it comes down to it, there is a key question to ask regarding both suppliers and buyers: Is there somebody who can knock on your door and dictate the price and terms of a transaction you need to make? From the supplier power perspective, can someone dictate what *you* will pay for a product or service? Limited supply options can happen because there are few suppliers, or it can occur because there is some rare skill or human asset you need. When the cast members of the popular TV sitcom *Friends* changed their negotiating style and negotiated as an actual group of inseparable friends, they took all the bargaining power away from the producers of the show.[9] If the producers wanted *Friends*, they had to buy all of them or get none. Given the incredible popularity of the show, the cast was clearly in the position of strength. Ask yourself if you have a key supplier or customer that can essentially dictate terms. If so, you need to think through how this might impact your ability to create value.

Threat of Substitutes

When considering your competitive position, it's important to realize that substitutes can be just as damaging to your potential for value creation as can direct competitors. If you're working in an industry influenced by technology or public policy—and virtually all industries are at this point—you need to be especially vigilant as you scan the competitive landscape. Substitute products and services often show up when technology adoption takes a leap forward or when public policy changes. The transportation industry is rich with examples. Twenty years ago, if you were a student looking to explore Europe on the cheap, the obvious choice among transportation options within Europe was Euro Rail. But that started to change when Europe deregulated its airline industry in the 1990s. Since then, several no-frills discount airlines like Ryanair and EasyJet have emerged, offering a low-cost alternative to train travel. But examples of substitution are equally abundant among small businesses. Lawyers must offer services that overcome the threat of substitute websites that offer self-service templates for legal documents. Similarly, accountants face substitution from software programs and online tax filing services.

Remember that sometimes substitutes can really come out of left field. Customers might choose to spend their money on something you never even thought could substitute for your offering. In the entertainment industry, for example, the product is really about how people choose to spend their leisure time. You might open a night club because none exists in your town, but you're not really competing against other night spots. You're competing against all those other leisure entertainment options. Take time to consider how customers might substitute other products or services for your own, or how you might offer a valuable substitute to attract customers from competitors.

Rivalry

To those of us who have played in the competitive marketplace, perhaps the most obvious of the five forces is the intensity of the rivalry in an industry. How fierce is the competition around you? Do your competitors have all the same strategic and tactical moves that you can offer? Will they match everything you do? Are the customers constantly bombarded with advertisements, offers to switch, price matching, promotional deals, and products or services just as good or better than yours? Do your competitors have deep pockets from which to fund their campaigns? Think about some of the industries around us in the world today. How much rivalry can you see in the cell phone market? That's one of the fastest-paced, intensely competitive markets in the world in which some of the largest companies of the world have been and will be humbled. How about the passenger vehicle market? Can you go for even one day without seeing advertisements for the latest, greatest cars with the latest, greatest promotional offers dangled in front of you? Considering just what kind of rivalry you will face is an important part of thinking about your external environment. All the market and non-market factors roll up together to influence how tough your rivalry will be, and you should understand that reality. In addition, the specific characteristics of certain companies can increase or decrease the rivalry you face. If you were about to start a business and knew that your two main competitors were going to be Apple and Google, might you hesitate to jump into that competitive sandbox?

Of course, sometimes the rivalry might help you rather than work against you. Established businesses—especially those aligned with industry groups operating nationally and internationally—tend to have well-formed political alliances, supportive services networks, suppliers, and so on. These networks provide a significant source of stability within whole industries and, often by their very design, form considerable obstacles for would-be rivals seeking to enter the market. Those obstacles might take the form of tight supplier relationships that limit newcomer access to resources, or the threat might be more political in nature. When disruptive new entrants like Uber come along in an industry as widespread and entrenched as taxi and car services, you can bet the established rivals are going to show up to defend their turf. The case study about Uber and Lyft provides more insight about Uber's rivalry with the hired-vehicle industry. Rivals can be fierce competitors, so be sure to consider whom you might find yourself up against in your market.

As you can see, none of these market and non-market factors in the external environment around you work independently of the others. It is all interrelated. The key is, as they say, to keep your eyes and ears open. The environment is rich with obstacles, but given the right resources and capabilities inside your organization, those obstacles might just become the source of your next innovation and lead to real value creation. With a better understanding of the factors influencing your external environment, let's shift our focus inside the organization to get a better understanding of the internal environment.

Looking Inside to Understand Your Internal Environment

If looking around at your external environment is like an adventure full of unexpected influences and nuanced social interactions, the internal assessment of the organizational environment is likely more quiet and introspective. Don't get me wrong. You may very well uncover some surprises, but as you look inside, you need to let down your guard a bit and open yourself up to whatever truths—however ugly they might be—the internal assessment has to show you. Brushing over long-standing issues doesn't get you the necessary understanding of your organization to really grasp your potential for value creation and your ability to sustain it over time. In your internal assessment, if you come across an issue, you need to dig deeper and try to understand what's really going on. If you are working with others, encourage candor so that you can gain deeper insights.

Above all, when seeking to understand your organization or your own personal situation, you must be honest with yourself. This is the time to look inside and allow yourself to really get to know your resources and capabilities. Why? Because some of them may just come together to form distinctive competencies—the very distinctive competencies that enable you to create value. So take a deep breath. Leave the external environment in the distance for a little while. Allow the clatter to fade, and prepare to listen. The internal environment has much to tell you. We will begin the discussion with a few tools that can help you hear well and gain a deeper understanding of your organization.

The Resource-Based View of Organizations

The resource-based view of organizations is a model for understanding your resources and capabilities and how they might come together to form distinctive competencies. Recall that I distinguish between core competencies—those things you do particularly well—and distinctive competencies. Our goal is to uncover distinctive competencies, those combinations of key resources and capabilities that are at once valuable and rare in the marketplace, and thus have potential for value creation. To get there, you must first understand—inventory, if you will—what it is you have with which to work. At this point in the V-REEL Framework, you've completed an initial inventory of your resources and capabilities. Using the resource-based view, you will expand your understanding of resources and capabilities. In doing so, you may discover you have some additional assets.

To begin, it is important to understand that resources come in two forms. The first you understand intuitively. Tangible resources are those things you first think of when I mention making an inventory. They are physical in nature such that you can see them and easily take stock. Included among your tangible resources are things like your labor, your physical space, equipment, supplies, capital, and so on. These are critical, but so, too, is the second class of resources. In fact, intangible resources are often more valuable than your tangible ones because they are often much more difficult to imitate. Intangible resources include those things that you cannot touch or see but may nonetheless have great value. Examples of intangible assets include your branding, knowledge, reputation, company culture, individual talents, and intellectual property. You can imagine how these might be incredibly valuable because, unlike tangible assets, which can often be imitated by the competition, intangibles can be much harder—if not impossible—to imitate. Think of the Disney brand. Yes, Disney has spent generations building its brand, and that longevity certainly plays into the brand's inimitability, but the intangible thing associated with the brand is the promise that is Disney. Happiness. Cherished memories. Wholesome family times. You can't touch that—literally or figuratively—but boy is it valuable!

Using the resource-based view of the firm, you are looking at what it is you have to work with—both the tangible and the intangible. Often organizations have a hard time seeing their own intangible resources. They struggle to recognize that it's actually the intangible but incredibly valuable customer service of one particular employee that keeps customers coming back. Or perhaps it is the vast personal and professional network of the CEO that really drives value creation. When developing your lists of resources—tangible and intangible—it is also useful to keep in mind that sometimes it is the combination of resources that really provides distinctiveness.

Google, for example, is at its core a company that develops web-based software applications. Clearly, Google is not just any software company. The company has amassed a suite of resources unlike almost any other company in the world. Google has tangible assets, of course: its headquarters complex, massive server farms, talented employees, and so on. But combine Google's physical assets with the Google brand, the social capital in Silicon Valley, unique knowledge and playful company culture, and now you have something really special. Google has created a very socially complex system of relationships with users and partners that is essentially impossible to replicate.

As you look at your internal environment, it is essential that you seek to identify both the tangible assets that contribute to your ability to create value and the intangible ones. This is not just an inventory. You must also ask if it's rare or if it has some degree of rareness. Given your previous exploration of the external environment, you should be better prepared to think about that question. Many strategists use the VRIS framework to think through resources and capabilities to begin to understand if they have anything that might be rare, and thus enable value creation.

The VRIS Framework

The VRIS framework is essentially a series of questions you can ask yourself about a resource or capability. This is to help you understand how potentially important it might be in your quest to create value. Figure 3: The VRIS Framework provides a graphical view of the framework. We begin by asking if the resource can create value. If so, move on to ask if it is rare and, if it is, then ask if it is inimitable. In other words, is it difficult to imitate? Finally, is it hard to substitute? Notice on the diagram that any time you are able to respond with yes, the process moves you forward toward a possible competitive advantage. But, if your response to any question is no, then the process prompts you to try again. Why? Because all aspects of the VRIS Framework are necessary to achieve the possibility of a competitive advantage. Even if something is difficult to imitate, it is still possible for a competitor to jump in and offer a substitute.

VRIS FRAMEWORK

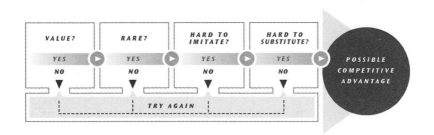

Figure 3: The VRIS Framework

This happens all the time. Consider how this happens with fast-food chains, for example. You might have the only fast-food option on the block, and you may even offer some healthy options that set your menu apart from other fast-food chains so people choose your restaurant over driving a bit further for a slightly healthier option. But a few months later, the local grocery store opens a new natural foods department complete with organic frozen meals for just about the same price as a meal deal at your restaurant—and just like that, a substitute is in a position to diminish your potential value creation. Even if it is difficult to imitate your product, you still must address that last question: Is it difficult to substitute?

Some may argue that if you can answer yes to all four questions, you have the makings of a sustained competitive advantage. I just cannot go quite that far. But I will say this: if you can work all the way through the VRIS filter answering yes at every stop along the way, you may very well be on to something. You may have a distinctive competency. And with that, we can work toward real value creation and perhaps a sustainable competitive advantage. For now, let's look at one more tool that might shed light on additional sources of value creation and potential distinctive competencies within your organization.

Developing a Competency Bundle

With the VRIS framework, we looked at individual resources and capabilities and sought to understand the extent to which they might contribute to your ability to create value. Even before the resource-based view and the VRIS framework came into use, Porter introduced Value Chain Analysis as the first way to look at the internal processes and capabilities employed while creating and delivering value. He called them primary and support activities. Value Chain Analysis is useful to help you think about activities you undertake; that's useful because activities are capabilities. Thinking through the capabilities you employ in the course of creating value can prompt you to recognize valuable competencies that might not otherwise come to mind. Porter's model traditionally includes thinking through a step-by-step series of activities related to things like supply chain management, operations, marketing, sales, service, and so on. Porter then references those primary activities being supported by activities such as human resource management, information systems, and procurement that are not directly related to the creation of products or services but are essential to running a business. A key insight taken from Porter's model is that all these activities—primary and supporting—are linked together in a chain to create value. What I'm asking you to do is take Porter's ideas a step further and think about how you can integrate your value–creating activities toward formation of distinctive competencies.

 Use the concept of a competency bundle to think about how you might combine resources, capabilities, and competencies to form something distinctive in your market.

The aim here is to understand how combining resources and capabilities might add value to the product or service, lower the cost of delivering it, or even create entirely new competencies. Doing so is useful because often it is here where you discover potential for real distinctive competencies hidden deep inside the operations of your organization. It is also possible that you might discover the opportunity for a distinctive competency that, given some additional investment or process improvement, could set you apart from the competition.

The exceptionally successful fast-food chain Chick-fil-A has combined customer service, organizational culture, and a unique franchising model to form something truly distinctive in the fast-food marketplace. Chick-fil-A combined capabilities and resources to form what I'm calling a "competency bundle." You can think about it much like a cable, which is really made up of a bundle of smaller cables. The binding together of the individual components creates something new that is potentially stronger and more durable, able to stand up to the forces of wear over time. Your competency bundle takes shape as you look at how you might weave together the activities you undertake as you work to create value. I want you to think about how those things are related to one another and could be integrated in a unique way such that, like the bundle of cables, the strength and durability of your combined resources and capabilities is far greater than the sum of the individual parts. Sometimes that's where magic happens. The way things are bound together into a competency bundle can lead to a distinctive competency.

Disney is a great example for understanding a competency bundle. Disney has great creative talent, but it also has a great marketing and distribution system, and the way that Disney marries that creative competency with marketing forms a strong distinctive competency. There are other companies that have great creative talent and others that have exceptional distribution, but few have those resources and capabilities so tightly woven together. Disney's competency bundle contributes to its distinctiveness in the marketplace. Figure 4: Developing a Competency Bundle provides a simple view of the competency bundle. You simply think about your resources, capabilities, and competencies and then step back and look for opportunities to weave them together into something far stronger. Let's walk through a not-for-profit example to get a sense of the various aspects of value chain analysis and the formation of competency bundles.

**DEVELOPING A
COMPETENCY BUNDLE**

Figure 4: Developing a Competency Bundle

If you're running a local theater company, your operations might include the following resources, capabilities, and competencies:

- Supply chain management—sourcing scripts, costumes, sets, lighting, and sound systems
- Operations—securing licenses for plays, scheduling rehearsals, set production, and performances
- Distribution—identifying locations for performances, establishing a season of performances
- Marketing and sales—promoting shows, establishing a website, selling tickets
- Service—customer support for ticket sales and guest services during shows, support for season ticket holders
- Research and development—researching potential plays, licensing fees
- Information systems—hiring a web developer and securing email services

- Human resources—hiring actors and production team members, training, securing employee benefits, and overseeing contract reviews
- Accounting and finance—managing ticket sales and donations, overseeing banking and accounts payable
- Processes, policies, and procedures—managing the board of directors, establishing hiring policies and ticketing procedures, forming fundraising strategies
- Talent—actors and actresses
- Production and design crews
- Social capital—your supporters, donors, and champions in the community
- Physical location

As the theater example shows, there is a lot that goes on behind the scenes of any organization. Profit margins occur when the value created through all an organization's activities exceeds the value expended to deliver it. In the case of our not-for-profit theater company, any profit margins would be invested back into the organization, perhaps for theater improvements or additional marketing. If it was a for-profit theater company, profits might be distributed among shareholders. In either case, profit margins are the goal, and we achieve those margins by differentiating our product or service such that we create more value than is required to deliver the product or service.

In analyzing the theater's resources, capabilities, and competencies, we may find that a major portion of tickets sales is directly attributed to the personal promotional activities of a board member. In the same review, we might discover that a staff member has been going the extra mile to make sure that the one proactive board member has all the resources she needs to sell tickets. That's an example of binding resources and capabilities to form a competency bundle. We discover that the board member and staff person have worked together to ensure a smooth sales process. The board member, the staff person, and the processes they established to get tickets sold, however informal, are creating significant value. They are also rare resources with rare capabilities, and woven together they form a distinctive competency that should be protected and, where possible, expanded.

Just as we walked through the hypothetical theater company to explore the workings of a hypothetical not-for-profit, you can use the resource-based view, the VRIS framework, and the competency bundle concept to help you take a close look at your own operations. Understanding your internal environment in light of the external environment opens your eyes to potentially valuable and rare resources and capabilities, as well as the potential for valuable combinations that you might otherwise overlook. If through consideration of your external and internal environments you discover additional distinctive competencies, be sure to add them to your inventory. Next, I will go a little deeper and present additional sources of rareness to consider in your hunt for distinctive competencies.

Additional Sources of Rareness

We've talked about the abilities of others to imitate your value and the ability of others to offer substitutes for your value. Those are the two big threats to rareness that strategy experts typically talk about in the resource-based view. Additionally, some of the things that have traditionally been considered barriers to entry into industries can influence the rareness of a product or service. Before I move on to rareness, let me first address this notion of barriers to entry because it is directly related to the degree of rareness you're likely to achieve. Generally, barriers to entry are not actually barriers at all. To say they are is to imply that a barrier to entry is something one cannot get around. That is simply not the case. Competitors can and do get around barriers to entry... eventually. Through the years, I've come to think of these things as speed bumps because you—and your competitors—*can* actually get over or past them. It may take time, and barriers or speed bumps may slow things down, but they won't stop the competition and shouldn't necessarily stop you from entering a competitive market.

Some examples of speed bumps are things like switching costs, economies of scale and scope, licensing, etc. Switching costs come into play when the cost to change is made high due to expenses associated with the change. For a customer to switch from your product to another product, there is more to consider than the price of the product: things like retraining, new hardware, and perhaps a need for new facilities. The switching costs are much more than the price of a competitor's product. So maybe high switching costs provide you a degree of rareness.

 Barriers to entry are more like speed bumps. They may slow things down, but they won't stop competitors and shouldn't necessarily stop you from entering a competitive market.

Economies of scale or economies of scope may also be a source of rareness. Efficiency, high volumes of production, or the breadth of the product line you produce may make you more productive than competitors. That makes you rare. Or maybe it's something like the network externality effect in the digital world where a larger user base makes you more valuable than anybody else. That user base becomes the thing that is rare. Social media is good example. What social media platform do you use? The one where you can connect to ten people, or the one where you can connect to ten *million* people?

There are different things that you can create that are very difficult for others to overcome for a variety of reasons. Maybe it's legal protection, such that you have a license to do something and no one else is going to get it because to do so would require an act of a governmental body. Maybe it's key relationships forming significant social capital. There are many different things that can serve to help make you rare while making it very difficult for others to have a shot at obtaining what you have. And that's the goal.

You seek rareness to accompany your value and enable you to create value. Without some degree of rareness, you simply cannot have a distinctive competency. Rareness is essential. Having gone through your resources and capabilities inventory, explored the external environment, and taken an honest look at the internal environment, you are equipped to answer the two essential questions to this point in the V-REEL Framework:

- Do I have something of value to offer in the marketplace?
- Is it rare?

If your answer to both questions is *yes*, great! You can move right on ahead through the rest of V-REEL and see how you might form a sound strategy for value creation. If you think you might have something rare but you're not quite sure, that's okay, too. Our next V-REEL topic will provide additional clarity and help uncover potential options for protecting the rareness you have and building additional resources and capabilities to bolster your rareness. But if you answered *no* to one or both questions, you may need to consider slowing down or stopping all together. Both value and rareness are essential for winning in the marketplace. As we move on to consider eroding factors, there is a chance we could still uncover opportunities for value and rareness. We will most certainly realize what resources and capabilities are most important to protect going forward.

Case Study: Value and Rareness in the Ride-Sharing Market

Through a quick internal and external analysis of Uber's global ride-service app, we can learn how value and rareness combine to form distinctive competencies in the marketplace. With the aim of simplifying the process of securing a ride, Uber founders, Travis Kalanick and Garrett Camp, leveraged both social and technological trends to bring a disruptive new ride service to an age-old industry. The pair launched Uber in the black car service sector in San Francisco in 2010. Looking at the external environment at the time, it's not surprising that we quickly see another player. Lyft was also getting started with a new app serving the City by the Bay, but unlike Uber, the Lyft app was an enhancement for a person-to-person ride share service that had been operating in the area since 2007.

Both Uber and Lyft were taking advantage of advances in technology. The advent of the smart phone—together with open-source models for mobile application development—paved the way for all manner of innovation by leveraging ubiquitous cellular networks. By 2008, Apple and Android had opened their app stores, and savvy entrepreneurs were toying with possibilities as they launched new downloadable-to-the-phone tools for the mobile consumer. And the consumer was ready. Socio-culturally speaking, the highly influential young-adult market—the same group that has never known life without a computer—was ready and willing to download apps for everything from entertainment to word processing. Apps that offered the opportunity to secure services directly from their smart phones would be a natural evolution of the user experience. Macro-economic factors were at play as well.

Super-low interest rates drove investors to new ventures resulting in vast amounts of investment capital. Uber raised $9 billion in equity and $1.6 billion in debt in just six years.[10] Meanwhile, the sluggish economy was teeming with individuals hungry for extra income. Uber read the market and went all in with a plan to win in San Francisco so it could move on to major markets around the world. The company primed the market by effectively subsidizing both driver compensation and rider fares until demand allowed for self-sustaining rates. The business model worked in San Francisco and Uber has duplicated the model around the globe. But the question remains. Is it rare? After all, Lyft is still out there.

Looking a little closer, two things seem to set Uber apart: First, and very significantly, the ability to attract major capital. Second, hard-core commitment to customer service. Uber sets high expectations for drivers, demanding efficiency and professionalism. Drivers are directed to open the car door, load luggage, and let customers ride in the back. By contrast, Lyft tried a more lighthearted approach, providing drivers with a huge pink mustache to mount on their vehicles and encouraging fist bumps with passengers. If monthly active user rates are an indication of customer satisfaction, the Uber approach seems to be winning. A full 89 percent of all U.S. users who used any car or ride-sharing app used Uber at least once during July 2016.[11] By contrast, 19 percent of the same population used Lyft. Still, other factors are coming into play and could threaten Uber's ability to create value.

Thinking about the political realm, among Uber's strongest opposition is the Taxicab, Limousine and Paratransit Association (TLPA),[12] an international industry association originally formed in 1917 to protect taxi operators from Federal government regulation and costly taxes. With one hundred years of government interactions under its belt, TLPA could be a formidable rival. The Association's congressional testimony and releases of formal statements are part of the group's ongoing international "Who's Driving You"[13] campaign.

Direct and intentional, the tagline leaves no doubt about TLPA's target. According to the website, Who's Driving You is a public safety campaign "Promoting for-hire vehicle safety and highlighting the risks of Uber and Lyft." Established in 2014, the website continues active attacks on Uber and Lyft. While, as of this writing, Uber continues strong with operations in more than five hundred cities worldwide, the company now must dedicate resources to address issues raised by rivals and battle legislation that would prevent operations in some locales.

Rivalries, legal and political factors, technological advancements, economic trends, and even ecological factors are all at play in Uber's external environment. Internally, Uber is building up more than a simple ride-sharing app. Instead, the company is building up its proven logistics resource and mapping capabilities to build additional value. Offerings like UberEATS for food delivery and UberPOOL for shared commuting as well as loyalty programs are all combining in a vast network of users and service partners. Both the network externality effect—the growing base of Uber users—and increasingly complex social relationships among Uber, drivers, and users are combining to form a rare competency bundle around the Uber model. Of course, there is no real way to predict the future of Uber, and it, too, must work to hone and protect distinctive competencies, but it is clear thus far that Uber succeeded in bringing both value and even some rareness to the growing sharing economy.

Key Steps and Useful Tools When Considering Value and Rareness

1. ARTICULATE YOUR VALUE PROPOSITION.
2. INVENTORY YOUR RESOURCES AND CAPABILITIES NEEDED TO CREATE VALUE.
3. CONSIDER YOUR EXTERNAL ENVIRONMENT.
   A. MARKET FACTORS
   B. NON-MARKET FACTORS
   C. BARGAINING POWER OF SUPPLIERS
   D. BARGAINING POWER OF BUYERS
   E. THREAT OF SUBSTITUTES
   F. THREAT OF NEW ENTRANTS
   G. RIVALRY
4. CONSIDER YOUR INTERNAL ENVIRONMENT.
   A. RESOURCE-BASED VIEW
   B. VRIS FRAMEWORK
   C. COMPETENCY BUNDLE
5. DOCUMENT POTENTIAL DISTINCTIVE COMPETENCIES (VALUABLE + RARE).

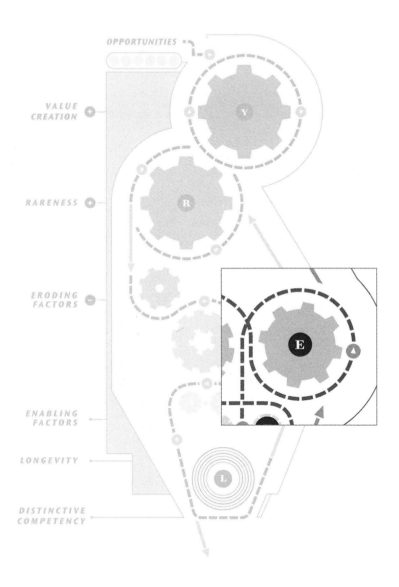

OPPORTUNITIES

VALUE
CREATION

RARENESS

ERODING
FACTORS

ENABLING
FACTORS

LONGEVITY

DISTINCTIVE
COMPETENCY

CHAPTER 3

Things That Go Bump
in the Night

You learned about the dangers of erosion in grade school. It's easy to find examples of the damaging effects of rain and wind; think of the banks of a creek eroding away in a particularly rainy season and cutting into your neighbor's back yard. That's bad. Or consider the devastating loss of lives and property resulting from landslides. Clearly, erosion is a destructive force in nature, and it can be equally damaging in the marketplace, degrading or destroying entirely your ability to create value or be rare. We need to understand erosion and how we might control it in order protect or at least prolong value creation and rareness.

In this chapter, we will look at the first *E* in the V-REEL Framework: Erosion. As we turn to this notion of erosion, or more accurately, erosion control, I will explain some of the more common causes of erosion and introduce the Erosion Matrix. The matrix will help you focus on those eroding factors that present the greatest threat to your ability to create value and be rare. All the work you've done so far to understand your external environment and your internal situation will serve you well as we move forward. Here, we are identifying vulnerabilities while prioritizing them according to potential impact. We do so to better understand our position in the market and where we might need to spend time and resources defending it. Let's get started. Let's take an honest look at potential eroding forces.

What Is Erosion?

Erosion, or an eroding factor, is anything that can hurt your ability to create value and/or take away your rareness. Threats to either potential value creation or rareness are of concern because both are necessary. If you do not have both, then you do not have anything distinctive to make you stand out in the marketplace. Anything that takes away from those two characteristics would be an eroding factor and something that you need to protect against to maintain or improve your position in the marketplace.

The two big threats from the resource-based view of the firm are imitation and substitution. We talked briefly about these in Chapter 2, but there are many other things beyond imitation and substitution that can actually erode your value and/or rareness. Some easy ones that come to mind are obsolescence or simple exhaustion of resources. Obsolescence can come from a variety of directions. For instance, there could be a technological shift, and suddenly the technology that is rare and value creating may still be rare but it no longer creates value. There is new technology that does the same thing differently or better. Are you old enough to remember Blockbuster Video? I loved strolling through the aisles of VHS tapes trying to decide to rent or buy. (I didn't, however, love the extra fees for not returning my rentals on time.) Blockbuster Video was great—until an easier, cheaper option came along. Today, video-rental stores are all but extinct, replaced by Redbox, Netflix, Amazon Video, Apple TV, and other services that allow us to peruse movie and TV options and enjoy instant access from virtually anywhere. Great for us. Not so great for Blockbuster.

 Erosion is a destructive force that can degrade or entirely destroy your ability to create value or be rare.

But obsolescence isn't always driven by technology. Demand patterns shift in society and change the market. Remember those sociocultural trends that we discovered in the external environment? The sharing economy, eco-friendly products, demand for healthy food options—these and countless other factors are at once opportunities for and potential threats to your ability to create value. In fact, all the environmental factors that we discussed in Chapter 2 as potentially contributing to your rareness in the market can also work against you, possibly eroding your ability to create value. You really must look at it both ways, first considering what you might have that's valuable and rare, and then almost immediately, considering what might erode away any potential distinctive competencies. You need to look at what is going on in the market and get real about your rareness by considering eroding factors. As a refresher, here's a quick list of some factors and trends mentioned in Chapter 2 that could erode your distinctive competencies.

- Politics, media, activism

- Macro-economic factors
- Sociocultural and demographic trends
- Technology
- Ecology
- Legal factors
- Global effects

Of course, the factors listed above are external. They are outside of the firm itself, but consider also erosion that could come from inside your organization. Changes in personnel, equipment, and processes could result in erosion of distinctive competencies, so it is important to consider internal factors as well as the external when considering potential erosion.

Okay. By now you might have a few questions: Why? Why am I still thinking and planning? I've gone to all this effort to understand the environment. I know my resources and capabilities. I have something of value and it's even rare. I have distinctive competencies! That's good enough. I don't need to read further. I'm good to go and ready to get on with my business.

Not so fast.

Remember the goal: create more value than you expend to create and deliver it. You're not seeking parity with the competition. You want to be better than the competition. You want to win in the marketplace. You're seeking a competitive advantage in your market and *perhaps* your distinctive competency offers you that. Great! You can, of course, go on out into the marketplace at this stage. Work hard. Tell the world about your amazing distinctive competency and make some money. But what's going to happen? If you don't consider erosion, the best you can hope for is parity with your competitors. At best, you'll be as good as everyone else, but your competition isn't going to like sharing customers with you, so something is going to happen. Before you know it, erosion will creep in—and just like that, you're underperforming. You're no longer on par with the competition. You've spent time and money to put yourself out there, but erosion is now eating away at profits.

 Remember the goal. You're not seeking parity with the competition. You want to be better than the competition. You want to win in the marketplace.

If you're pitching an idea to an executive or investors, it is very likely they already understand erosion, even if they don't use that term. By reeling in your enthusiasm for just a few minutes and taking the time to think through things that might chip away at your potential value creation and rareness, you will prepare a much stronger pitch. Erosion, if left unconsidered or unchecked, will get the best of your business. You must seek ways to control the eroding factors that are the greatest threat to your value and rareness.

To help identify the eroding factors of most concern, my colleagues and I created the Erosion Matrix. This simple tool is designed to help you determine what, if anything, can be done to defend against those factors most threatening to your potential value creation. If your neighbor had realized that the storm waters were going to wash away his property, he would have done what he could to stabilize the soil and protect his investment. You can do the same here once you take the time to understand what might erode your potential value and rareness.

The Erosion Matrix

Figure 5: The Erosion Matrix for Competencies will help you think about the factors that might undermine your distinctive competencies. Let's walk through it quickly. To begin, list your potential distinctive competencies. You may find it useful to number each one for later reference. Remember, distinctive competencies are both valuable and rare. Perhaps it is your location on the main thoroughfare in town, your lean supply chain, the special skills of an employee, or a competency bundle of reputation and personal network. When making your own matrix, remember to think about the tangible and intangible resources, capabilities, competencies, and competency bundles that are both valuable and rare. A blank copy of the Erosion Matrix for Competencies is available in the Resources section of this book and online at ThinkBeyondValue.com.

EROSION MATRIX FOR COMPETENCIES

ITEM	DISTINCTIVE COMPETENCY ⊕	ERODING FACTOR ⊖ Works against distinctive competency	LIKELIHOOD Scale of 1–10, with 10 being currently exists or certain to occur	IMPACT Scale of 1–10, with 10 having profound and significant impact on the organization	EROSION RATING Likelihood multiplied by impact

Figure 5: The Erosion Matrix for Competencies

Once you've listed your distinctive competencies, it's time to consider eroding factors. What might happen to take away or devalue the benefits of your location? Could something hurt your reputation? What if that especially skilled employee leaves the company? For each distinctive competency in your matrix, take the time to think about and list the things that could happen. Include your team and encourage open, candid discussion. There could be only a few eroding factors, or you might think of many things that could erode your distinctive competencies and are potential threats to your distinctiveness. You can't address vulnerabilities you're not aware of, so this is time well spent.

Once you have a good, solid list of eroding factors for each of your distinctive competencies, you may find yourself a bit discouraged. If your list of eroding factors is long, you might be wondering if, or how, you can overcome so much erosion. The truth is, you probably can't. But that might be okay. The next two columns in the matrix will help you see a bit more clearly the eroding factors about which you really need to be concerned. Using a simple scoring system, we are going to quantify how critical each eroding factor might be. In doing so, you will prioritize each eroding factor so you can focus your efforts to protect distinctive competencies. Moving on to the next two columns, you ask yourself two questions about each eroding factor on your list: First, how likely is it to happen? Second, how impactful would it be if it did?

To keep it simple, we use a basic scoring range of one to ten, with ten being most likely or most devastating. Go ahead and fill in those two columns, answering each question for each item on your list of eroding factors. By now you have done a lot of work, and you're quite familiar with both your external environment and internal situation, so go with your gut sense of the ranking for each item. The rankings are, of course, relative and subjective, but they support the prioritization process nonetheless. If you've done a good job of identifying potential distinctive competencies and potential eroding factors, your rating of each factor will work to expose items of greatest concern. You will begin to see where you need to focus your strategic efforts going forward.

With rankings noted for each eroding factor, you can calculate the erosion rating by multiplying the likelihood estimate by the impact estimate. Do this for each of the eroding factors. The factors with the highest erosion ratings are the most critical. These are the factors that, left unchecked, could be the most devastating to your ability to create value or maintain rareness. Let's quickly walk through an example to demonstrate the power of the Erosion Matrix to focus your strategy formulation.

Bigger and Better

Buc-ee's is a chain of rest stop convenience stores across Texas that makes good on the promise that everything is bigger in the Lone Star State. Buc-ee's initial claim to fame was the nicest and cleanest restrooms on the road. While we can all agree that clean convenience store restrooms are valuable and rather rare, it is a competency that can and has been replicated. Buc-ee's anticipated erosion of that competency and bundled it with other distinctive competencies to stand out in the marketplace. Looking at Figure 6: Buc-ee's Erosion Matrix for Competencies, we see that in addition to nice, clean restrooms, the chain also offers a wide variety of quality food and retail products, and Buc-ee's works to ensure staff members are friendly. Food and retail products are still rather replicable, although Buc-ee's does offer exclusively branded products. But look at the last item on the list of distinctive competencies: "fun, wholesome brand and experience." Customer experiences are one of those intangible and emotionally satisfying competency bundles that can be quite difficult to replicate, and therefore, can become a very strong distinctive competency.

EROSION MATRIX: BUC-EE'S

ITEM	DISTINCTIVE COMPETENCY	ERODING FACTOR	LIKELIHOOD Scale of 1–10, with 10 being currently exists or certain to occur	IMPACT Scale of 1–10, with 10 having profound and significant impact on the organization	EROSION RATING Likelihood multiplied by impact
1	Consistently clean restrooms	Imitation—other chains with the same	8	5	40
		Failure to have predictably clean restrooms	8	7	56
2	Wide variety of food and product	Imitation—other chains with the same	6	6	36
3	Friendly staff	Decline in quality of staff/training	4	7	28
4	Fun wholesome brand and experience	Imitation—other chains with the same	4	9	36
		Loss of image and quality of experience	2	10	20

Figure 6: Buc-ee's Erosion Matrix for Competencies

Since launching in 1982, Buc-ee's has been building a unique brand of Texas-style wholesome fun packaged up and delivered at more than two dozen of the most sought-out convenience stores in the state. The chain has enjoyed great success, but even Buc-ee's needs to guard against erosion. If Buc-ee's fails to consistently offer clean restrooms, customers will have much less reason to stop. And if customers stop coming, no amount of fun branding matters. Everything falls apart from there. The high erosion rating tells us that clean restrooms are clearly something Buc-ee's must protect if it hopes to sustain its distinctive competency. But keep in mind, while clean restrooms are necessary, critical even, to Buc-ee's model, they are not sufficient for competitive advantage. The whole Buc-ee's customer experience, including a wide variety of food and retail products, is also essential. Ultimately, it is the whole customer experience, including clean restrooms, that combines in a competency bundle to form the brand that so powerfully distinguishes Buc-ee's in the convenience store market and enables it to create considerable value.

A Different Kind of Thinking

Just as Buc-ee's distinctive competencies combine to form a powerful experience for consumers, major players in the business-to-business marketplace also combine distinctive competencies to build strong brands. Once famous for typewriters and even personal computers, IBM is among the world's top players in the business-to-business technology sector. Over time, new entrants moved into the typewriter and personal computer markets. Imitation and eventually obsolescence eroded away Big Blue's ability to create value with technology alone. But after more than one hundred years, one thing the tech giant seems to do well is reinvent itself; IBM didn't make it to the rare centenarian class of businesses without identifying eroding factors and developing new distinctive competencies that have served it over the decades. What are those distinctive competencies?

Early IBM leader Thomas J. Watson established the company's motto,[14] and his successors have shaped "Think" into an organizational culture that has become a distinctive competency. Today, IBM ranks among the top problem solvers in the world. Rather than focus on a single technology, the company has managed to hold on to its mantra, establishing a company culture focused on providing solutions to customer problems and, through that, building a trusted brand. IBM works across industry sectors as a solutions provider, bringing both innovative thinking and technology, touching every major industry across the globe. Still, eroding factors have taken their toll over the years.

By the 1990s, IBM had lost sight of the customer and was relying largely on mainframe computer sales. Heavy on technology and light on problem solving, erosion in the form of technological change was a real threat. Mainframes were being replaced by personal computers. Louis Gerstner took the reins in 1993 and returned the company's focus to its fundamental ability to solve customer problems. To ensure that IBM could do that on a large scale, Gerstner reversed plans to break apart the company. He understood that IBM's collective technology expertise and array of business activities combined synergistically to form something rare and valuable to corporate and government customers. He recognized the distinctive competency bundle, how breaking up the components would erode the company's ability to create value and took steps to stop the erosion.

 The companies that stand the test of time have a pattern of recognizing eroding factors early and responding. They use enabling resources and capabilities to bolster rareness and curtail or put off erosion of value.

As you might expect, Gerstner is not the only IBM executive over the company's long history to step in and put measures into place to keep erosion at bay and restore distinctiveness. Using distinctive competencies to sustain competitive advantage in the market is actually quite rare. Some argue that it simply does not exist in the long run. In reality, if you look at the history of any company with any substantial longevity, you find that erosion has taken hold at some point, resulting in periods of parity or even competitive disadvantage before the company worked back to a position of competitive advantage. The companies that stand the test of time have a pattern of recognizing eroding factors early or, at the very least, responding well to them with enabling resources and capabilities that bolster rareness and curtail or put off erosion of value. This pattern of response positions companies to stand the test of time. With that understanding well established, let's move on to the next *E* in the V-REEL Framework: Enabling Factors. These are the things that can work *against* erosion and *with* distinctive competencies to extend your ability to create value and be rare in the marketplace. We will learn more about enabling factors in Chapter 4.

Case Study: The Eroding Away of Blockbuster Video

Between 1985 and 2010, Blockbuster Video was a household name. Families across the country "[Made] it a Blockbuster Night," visiting the local movie rental house to grab the latest release or an old classic before returning home with all the makings of a cozy family night in. Ask anyone on the street what happened to bring Blockbuster down and the person will likely suggest that technology changed and got the best of Blockbuster. Certainly, obsolescence was a factor, but a closer look at the Blockbuster story sheds light on eroding factors that came into play over twenty-five years of the movie rental business, and how Blockbuster's success ebbed, flowed, and ultimately dried up.

Looking back, we can identify several distinctive competencies that made Blockbuster the leader in video, and later, DVD rentals. We can also see where erosion sometimes took hold, resulting in periods of dramatic declines in profit.[15] The Blockbuster story started when founders David and Sandy Cook set out to sell take-out entertainment to American families. Blockbuster's colorful branding and clean, well-organized video stores combined to create a wholesome experience. By the late 1980s, family movie night was born. What are the distinctive competencies at play here?

On the tangible side, we have bright, colorful, and clean stores with vast libraries of videos available for rent. The intangible brand is also a distinctive competency: the bundling of positive in-store experiences and advertising that reinforced Blockbuster's role in wholesome family nights. Blockbuster also figured out the logistics of acquiring videos from distributors in a timely fashion. Those systems and the supplier relationships were also distinctive competencies. And not to be overlooked, the founders' focused commitment to the mission of delivering take-home family entertainment also revealed itself as perhaps Blockbuster's single most important distinctive competency.

That's a pretty healthy list of the distinctive competencies that set Blockbuster apart in the market. What are the associated eroding factors? Stores with shelves full of videos available for rent can be replicated. In fact, Hollywood Video did replicate the Blockbuster model and did well enough that Blockbuster spent considerable resources on an acquisition bid for Hollywood Video that ultimately failed. Meanwhile, a groundswell of other eroding factors was about to wreak havoc. DVDs were taking the place of VHS tapes and opening the door for Netflix's convenient mail-order alternative to Blockbuster's storefront. Even before Netflix came on the scene, cable and satellite companies offered movies on demand. The rush of substitute products and direct competitors was eroding Blockbuster's ability to deliver family entertainment. As you might expect, dramatic declines in market share prompted leadership changes, but in the case of Blockbuster, those changes didn't always work out well. And that brings us to the intangible but ever-so-important distinctive competency that, in the case of Blockbuster Video, was its focus on the customer.

When Blockbuster leadership kept the company focused on the original mission of delivering family entertainment, business flourished. But a few leaders in the company's history saw Blockbuster differently and shifted focus to a retail model. Resources shifted away from offering great entertainment to maximizing revenue per square foot. Customers were not interested in retail products and profits plummeted. Add Blockbuster's late-fee policy to the misguided focus on retail, and gradually Blockbuster lost its luster. While late fees accounted for as much as $400 million in annual revenue,[16] they proved a major customer turnoff. By 1997, erosion of customer satisfaction combined with an abundance of substitutes brought Blockbuster to the brink of collapse. Netflix wasn't even on the scene yet, and Blockbuster was already in trouble.

John Antioco, known for his turnaround of Circle-K and Taco Bell, offered fresh insight, essentially returning Blockbuster's focus to customers' desire for entertainment. During his ten years with the company, which began in 1997, Antioco made the bold move to eliminate late fees and forged an industry-disrupting deal with Hollywood studios, sharing rental revenues and ensuring that Blockbuster had an ample supply of popular movies.[17] The Blockbuster Guarantee meant customers were once again going home happy. The company's stockholders were happy, too. But Antioco was aware of changing technology and new platforms for delivering entertainment, all of which threatened to erode the company's position in the market.

In answer to the fledging Netflix, Antioco launched Blockbuster's Total Access program, allowing Blockbuster customers to order movies online for home delivery and return them to the stores. He also began leveraging the company's studio relationships to package

Blockbuster On Demand movies for cable companies. The timing wasn't always perfect, but Antioco and his team were laser focused on the customer and forming new models and networks to deliver entertainment. So what happened? Did Blockbuster, in fact, wait too long to play against Netflix's online offering? I don't think so. Here's why: by 2006, Blockbuster's five thousand stores and the online Total Access program were serving fifty million customers. Netflix had only four million customers[18] and nowhere near enough capital to build a brick and mortar presence. Neither Netflix nor Hollywood could rival Blockbuster's distinctive competency of delivering entertainment in-store and online, but that didn't mean erosion couldn't come into play from another direction. And it did, with a vengeance.

Sometimes erosion comes from within. Recall Blockbuster's intangible distinctive competency we called customer focus? Customer focus is a function of leadership. When a nasty spat over executive compensation left Blockbuster without a CEO, the board brought on a new leader who reverted to a retail model. He filled the stores with lots of products that had very little to do with family movie night. The same leader was so convinced of his retail vision that he managed to alienate the very team that had built Blockbuster's customer loyalty both in store and online during the previous decade. The entire executive team was gone within ninety days and, without them, Blockbuster's hard-earned distinctive competencies washed away. Within eighteen months of Antioco's exit, Blockbuster lost 85 percent of its market capitalization.[19] Shareholders lost millions, but Netflix had an opportunity. As is always the case, the same forces that erode distinctive competencies in one business context form potential for new competency in another business context; thus, Netflix is today a household name in entertainment, while Blockbuster is reduced to a case study. Erosion is powerful. It can be swift. But understanding eroding factors and building up defenses against them can mean the difference between short runs of success and long-term gains.

Key Steps and Useful Tools When Considering Erosion

1. BEGIN WITH YOUR POTENTIAL DISTINCTIVE COMPETENCIES (VALUABLE + RARE).

2. CONSIDER POTENTIAL ERODING FACTORS FOR EACH DISTINCTIVE COMPETENCY.

    A. CONSIDER IMITATION, SUBSTITUTION, OBSOLESCENCE, DEPLETION, ETC.

    B. CONSIDER NON-MARKET FACTORS AS SOURCES OF EROSION (POLITICAL, SOCIOCULTURAL, ETC.).

    C. CONSIDER MARKET FACTORS AS SOURCES OF EROSION (EQUIPMENT COSTS, AVAILABLE LABOR , ETC.).

3. COMPLETE THE EROSION MATRIX.

    A. LIST POTENTIAL DISTINCTIVE COMPETENCIES.

    B. LIST POTENTIAL ERODING FACTORS FOR EACH DISTINCTIVE COMPETENCY.

    C. RATE THE LIKELY OCCURRENCE OF EACH FACTOR.

    D. RATE THE POTENTIAL IMPACT OF EACH FACTOR.

    E. CALCULATE YOUR EROSION RATINGS.

4. NOTE EROSION FACTORS WITH THE HIGHEST EROSION RATINGS.

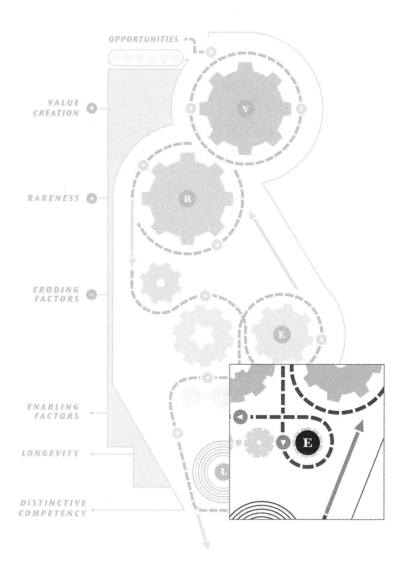

OPPORTUNITIES

VALUE
CREATION

RARENESS

ERODING
FACTORS

ENABLING
FACTORS

LONGEVITY

DISTINCTIVE
COMPETENCY

CHAPTER 4

When the Going Gets Tough

L iving in Texas, I've learned that the weather can change at a moment's notice. Such was the case for a friend of mine when she stopped at the HEB grocery store before meeting guests at her house. She was in a hurry, so she stopped at the store on the way home rather than go out of her way to her usual store. All was well on the way in, but as she headed to the doors with a cart full of groceries, the bottom fell out of the sky and there was no longer a dry path to the car. She immediately started weighing her options. Arrive late or arrive soaking wet. She really didn't want to endure the pelting rain so she reached for her phone and prepared to beg forgiveness. Before she had the chance, a young man interrupted her text message with the offer of a giant umbrella. HEB to the rescue! Not only did the young man look after her cart full of groceries while she made her way to the car, he was prepared upon her return with another umbrella, holding it over the trunk and her head as she loaded the groceries.

As she drove away, mostly dry and on time, she noticed a manager coming out to check on his employees. He had rubber boots for the umbrella handlers and was thanking them for their efforts. What's going on here? Enabling of value creation. When the going gets tough, the tough get enablers. Grocery stores cannot compete on price so they must do something else to keep their distinction in the marketplace. The extra effort with the umbrellas made my friend feel cared for. When was the last time you felt that way in a grocery store? HEB is building a distinctive competency around the customer experience and, based on my friend's time shopping on one really rainy evening in Texas, that store is doing a great job of enabling the distinctive competency. How? By paying attention to small details that add up to exceptional customer service.

 There are two types of enabling factors: those directly related to defending against erosion, and general enablers of organizational operations.

As you were identifying eroding factors threatening each of your distinctive competencies, you probably very naturally started thinking of ways to defend against erosion. As you did so, you were moving into the consideration of enabling factors. It's intuitive. You know you need to put mechanisms into place to stop erosion of your value and rareness so you can maintain some degree of distinction in the marketplace. When prompted, you probably also recognize that there are additional resources and capabilities unrelated to erosion control that you need to have in place to run your organization. So, in essence, there are two types of enabling factors: those directly related to defending against erosion and general enablers of organizational operations. Both are required for value creation. When HEB decided to offer umbrellas and extra service to customers during not-uncommon Texas storms, it was enabling its distinctive competency in customer service. HEB is defending against erosion of the customer experience using umbrellas which are not rare or distinctive. They are just umbrellas. But they are bundled with an organizational culture and service mindset that are valuable, rare, and form a distinctive competency.

When Blockbuster's Antioco established the revenue-sharing relationships with Hollywood studios, he was doing so to defend against eroding customer satisfaction brought on by Blockbuster's low available stock of popular films. The studio relationships were an enabling factor, which, by the way, became a new distinctive competency over time. It is not uncommon for new distinctive competencies to emerge as you build up enablers. But we know that Blockbuster had other enablers in place to support operations; for example, as a publicly traded company, Blockbuster had significant accounting resources in place. But Blockbuster was not in the accounting business. The accounting capability was not necessary to defend against any specific eroding factor. But accounting is a necessary capability to enable operations and is necessary for supporting value creation.

You need to consider both types of enabling factors. First, consider those enabling factors that defend against erosion of distinctive competencies. Once you are certain you can put measures into place to shore up or extend the life of distinctive competencies, you will consider what additional enabling resources are required to create value. There are almost always some additional resources and capabilities needed to make an organization work. You need to spend a bit of time making sure you cover all your bases so you can form a solid plan. But be careful here. Enabling factors are important; they are even critical. You must have them. But it is essential that in considering enabling resources and capabilities you do not forget how you create value and remain rare in the marketplace. You must not lose sight of your distinctive competencies. All these things—distinctive competencies and enablers—are necessary for the functioning of your organization, but for you to be successful you must know what your distinctive competencies are and keep the entire organization focused on supporting them.

I offer this cautionary note because there are potentially a lot of enabling factors. You can, and perhaps should, spend quite a bit of time considering your enablers. There may be a number of far-reaching considerations wrapped up in them. With so much to think through, it can be easy to run down a rabbit trail and forget what you were trying to accomplish in the first place. As I talk about enabling factors in this chapter, I will touch on a lot of strategic management topics and, depending on your organization and goals, you may determine that you need to look further into some areas. That's all good. But always remember to circle back to value and rareness and those distinctive competencies that will set you apart in the marketplace. And always remember that it is the resources and capabilities that are rare and valuable that form the competencies you are working to build up and protect. The manager at HEB came to check on his umbrella handlers because, when a Texas storm hits, those umbrella handlers are HEB's most valuable players. They're working on the front lines of customer experience. The manager understood this well and was paying attention to enabling his distinctive competency. The V-REEL Framework, by looping you back to value and rareness, can help keep you focused as you work through consideration of erosion and enabling factors to build and execute a stronger strategy.

In this chapter, I will focus on enabling factors in hopes of offering you a deeper understanding of the relationship between eroding factors and enabling factors, and your ability to create value. Here you will begin to experience the power of the V-REEL Framework as its recursive design prompts you to consider and reconsider various aspects of value creation in an intuitive process that refines big ideas into sustainable business strategy. So, let's get on with our discussion of enabling factors. I will begin by looking at those factors that defend against erosion of value and rareness.

Enabling Factors for Erosion Control

As we consider the enabling factors required to make your big idea a reality and create value in the marketplace, we return to the Erosion Matrix. Recall that we calculated an erosion rating for each identified eroding factor. Those factors with the highest erosion ratings are most critical. We need to determine what, if any, enabling factors we can put into place to keep erosion from destroying distinctive competencies. If customer service is a distinctive competency, then good human resource (HR) capabilities are an enabling factor. Without strong HR making good hiring decisions, delivering effective training programs, and monitoring employee performance, customer service will very likely suffer. If you've identified exceptional customer service as a distinctive competency, you need to plan on building up the enabling resources and capabilities of an exceptional HR office.

The popular food chain Chick-fil-A is known for exceptional customer service. What's behind that distinctive competency that has customers coming back for more? As you might expect, every employee is trained in customer service. But I think it is safe to assume every fast-food chain in the country provides employees with some amount of customer service training. Chick-fil-A, however, takes customer service to a whole new level and it seems to be paying off. With sales in excess of $6 billion in 2015,[20] the chain earns more per store in the six days it is open each week than McDonald's does in seven days. Chick-fil-A helps employees understand that a restaurant is a place of restoration, so the company and employees adopt an attitude of hospitality and strive to treat people better than the place down the street. The company achieves an exceptional level of service and associated customer loyalty by first being loyal to employees and empowering them to go the extra mile to provide exceptional customer service. Chick-fil-A hourly employees set their own hours (within limits) and every employee earns a $1,000 college scholarship.[21] With employee turnover at one-third the industry average[22] and as the only restaurant named to 24/7 Wall Street's 2014 Customer Service Hall of Fame,[23] it is clear Chick-fil-A has strong enabling factors protecting the quality of the chain's customer service.

What are some other common eroding factors and value-defending enablers? If you're like Uber and your business model is dependent on ride-share-friendly local laws, then you're going to need lobbyists working on your behalf to protect the feasibility of your business model. Walmart depends on store shelves well-stocked with the low-priced goods customers want. To make sure it delivers, the world's largest retailer has developed one of the world's largest private sales databases and supply chain logistics system. Facebook and Google rely on talented techies to continuously deliver online innovations and keep their sites up and running in real time. Despite the high stress of product launches and the demands of 24/7 operations, the tech giants were ranked first and second in Business Insider's 2015 list of Best Companies to Work for in America.[24] Both companies understand that keeping talented human resources happy at work is critical to value creation and so have established strong benefits packages and a dynamic work environment as enabling factors working against erosion in the form of employee turnover.

By now you're probably asking yourself what you need to put into place to defend against erosion of your distinctive competencies. Return to your Erosion Matrix for Competencies and ask what enabling resources or capabilities might you put into place to keep eroding factors from hurting your value creation and rareness? And thinking of it from a different angle, how might you approach your market differently than the competition to set yourself apart?

When Sam Walton was starting up Walmart in the 1960s, he faced direct competition from both Target and K-MART. Walmart did some very interesting things that enabled it to grow. First, Walmart didn't compete head-to-head with the others. It located Walmart stores in smaller towns away from big metropolitan areas. Walmart was using geography to its advantage by locating in places where there were no competitors and establishing its big-box stores as the place to shop. Second, Walton focused on being the everyday low-price leader. He determined that Walmart would do everything it possibly could to have the lowest prices. From the very beginning, Walmart invested huge amounts in logistics; it made sure its information systems and supply chain enabled its low price distinctive competency.

Clearly, most organizations are not and never will become as large as Walmart, but the lessons apply to any size organization. Sam Walton understood his external environment; he knew his distinctive competency and he built up enabling capabilities and resources to defend against erosion of Walmart's position as the low-cost and low-price leader. Given your distinctive competencies and understanding what forces might erode them away, you can think through what resources and capabilities you might put in place to control erosion. Keep in mind that the more tangible your enabling capabilities and resources are, the easier they will be for competitors to replicate. Tangible resources and capabilities can be seen, touched, and measured. They are, therefore, more easily understood and replicated. As a result, your investment in enabling factors may only gain you short-term defense against erosion because your competitors are very likely to come along and do the same thing you just did, bringing everyone back to competitive parity. Target followed Walmart's lead and invested significantly in logistics and supply chain to compete more effectively against its discount rival. As a result, the two largely strive to maintain parity.

 The more tangible your enabling capabilities and resources are, the easier they will be for competitors to see and to replicate.

While tangible and observable resources and capabilities like logistics systems can be easy to replicate, intangibles are often very difficult for competitors to copy. They are often better enablers defending against erosion. Chick-fil-A outperforms competitors in the fast-food market largely because it places so much emphasis on protecting the intangible—but extremely valuable—customer experience. And because it is intangible, it is much more difficult for competitors to replicate. As you're thinking through potential enabling factors to defend against erosion, be sure to consider both tangible and intangible approaches. Table 2: Enabling Factors for Erosion Control—Tangible and Intangible offers some eroding factors and both tangible and intangible enabling resources and capabilities that may help control erosion of distinctive competencies. Use these examples to help you begin thinking of enablers that might work to stop erosion of your own distinctive competencies.

Distinctive Competency	Eroding Factor	Tangible Enablers	Intangible Enablers
Only French restaurant in town	New entrant in market; substitute	Loyalty program, daily specials	Training / HR program to enable exceptional customer service
Easy-to-use, affordable private car service	City regulators threaten your existence	Lobbyists to monitor legislation to defend right to operate	Popular with voters; friendly with city council
Best jazz band in town	Drummer thinking about moving away	Pay drummer more; have back-up drummer	Reputation as best jazz band in town; talent wants to play with you
Best known not-for-profit children services program in town	Reduction in government funding	Develop private donor base	Reputation for good stewardship; social capital from strong community relationships
Most experienced web design team in town	Locals can hire out of town expertise for same service	Advertise the fact that business is local and can meet face to face	Good customer experience; strong local reputation; local social capital
Easily accessible location for personal service business	Competitor moves to equally accessible location	More advertising; loyalty program	Create superior customer experience
Prime location in mall	Anchor tenant moves away	Consider better location	Strong brand with customer following; work with other mall tenants to boost attraction of mall

Table 2: Enabling Factors for Erosion Control—Tangible and Intangible

Enabling Organizational Operations

Having identified enabling factors to defend against erosion of distinctive competencies, you are ready to turn your attention to the additional resources and capabilities you may need in place to deliver value. Returning to the list of distinctive competencies in the Erosion Matrix for Competencies, you probably recognize that these competencies do not represent the whole picture of your organizational strategy. There are other things you need to consider and perhaps additional resources and capabilities required to enable value creation. So how do we get at those other things? How do we figure out what we need to have in place to deliver value? These are potentially very big questions, and there is no single answer except to say, it depends. When considering enabling factors for your organization, the things you need to consider will vary depending on the scope of your operation, your location, and many other factors. What we are really doing when considering enabling factors is taking on many of the broader questions of traditional strategic management. You're working to improve and streamline your functional-level strategies, like improving your accounting operations or HR department, for example. You're also considering business-level strategy. Should you focus on cost leadership or try to be a differentiator? If you're a larger organization with multiple businesses, you might need to consider your corporate-level strategy to improve synergy across different types of businesses. If you're working internationally, you may need to think about enabling the appropriate mix of localization versus standardization. But clearly, all these things do not apply to all organizations.

Considering Operational Strategies

My challenge to you is to think beyond value, which includes considering the enabling factors required to support your operations. Keeping in mind what you know from your work thus far with the V-REEL Framework—your distinctive competencies, eroding factors, and even some enabling factors to defend against erosion—let's turn to organizational strategy. If you understand what your general approach to value creation will be, that may help you determine what additional enabling resources and capabilities you will need to put in place. In the field of strategic management, there is a lot of discussion, research, and writing about cost leadership and differentiation as two general strategies for creating value in the marketplace. From a theoretical perspective, these are fine and good categories. It is useful to discuss these two general approaches to value creation and try to identify the enabling factors required to support them. But in real-world practice—where competition is rampant—it is just not realistic to think that you only need to focus on cost, or you only need to focus on differentiation. If you want to compete, you must manage costs *and* you must, at least to some degree, differentiate yourself. Still, given your situation, one might be more critical than the other, but that doesn't mean you get to ignore the other. And organizations, big and small, make that mistake all the time.

Walmart suffered for a time back in the 1990s because it went too far with cost reductions and trying to maximize revenue per square foot. The retailer did away with greeters and overcrowded the stores with racks and racks of product. The experience was diminished to the point that customers sought out better shopping experiences with other discount retailers. Sales suffered and Walmart realized it had taken the cost leadership strategy a bit too far. It lost sight of the customer experience and suffered the market consequences. Certainly, Walmart doesn't need to offer the retail experience of a high-end department store, but it can't neglect the customer experience altogether. And if you're thinking cost leadership is a model you want to pursue, you also must keep the customer in mind even as you work to keep costs down. Knowing this, what might you need to be thinking about in terms of enablers for cost leadership?

Retailers like Walmart and Target enable their cost leadership strategies by bringing the same or similar value for customers as might be provided by the competition, but they reduce the cost of doing so and pass the savings on to the customer. To influence costs, managers operating under a cost leadership strategy must monitor cost drivers and work to keep costs low. To do so, they monitor the costs of inputs, such as raw materials, capital, and labor. They might enable low costs by establishing special contracts with suppliers or through bulk purchasing—all with the aim of gaining a cost advantage over competitors. Kia is a Korean car manufacturer with models that compete directly with some GM cars. The value offered is comparable across the two brands, but Kia's cars tend to be produced at lower cost. Kia enjoys some advantages over GM due to lower labor costs in Korea, for example, while some small businesses enjoy lower labor costs by employing young family members. Whatever the approach, any organization seeking to operate under a cost leadership model will need enablers in place to reduce costs of inputs.

Organizations developing a cost leadership strategy should also keep in mind that cost leadership can be difficult to achieve and perhaps even more difficult to maintain. Typical enabling factors aimed at driving costs down—such as robust logistics, economies of scale, and manufacturing efficiencies—are tangible, and thus can be replicated by competitors. And that's the very reason that cost leadership alone as a strategy is just not enough to create real value in the marketplace over the long term. Even as a cost leader, to win customers, you probably need some level of differentiation beyond low price.

What does differentiation strategy look like, and how might you enable it? The fundamental objective of a differentiation strategy is for your customers to believe that your goods or services are more valuable than your competitors' based on some unique product feature or quality. Of course, costs remain a factor for the manager seeking differentiation. The key to competitive advantage here is to ensure that any additional value created exceeds any increased costs. This is important to keep in mind because, naturally, there are usually costs associated with differentiation. Say a company wants to differentiate itself from the competition based on quality. The cost of quality materials required to make quality products is going to be a factor. Similarly, if an organization chooses to differentiate based on exceptional customer experience, there are going to be costs associated with the hiring and training of employees, with experience creation, and so forth.

You might be wondering how it is possible to achieve a distinctive competency with a differentiation strategy. The key here is customer perception of value. If you are a marketing person, you understand customer perception. If you have marketing people around you, they will probably just nod knowingly when you share this insight. With differentiation, customer perception of value will make or break the deal. And remember, the customer defines value. Luxury cars provide good examples of differentiation and perceived value. For someone who might purchase a Porsche, racing performance is expected and luxury features like fine leather, wood finishes, and premium sound systems are valuable. But even more valuable is the image and exclusivity associated with owning a Porsche. After all, not everyone can afford a Porsche. Maybe Porsche spends more to produce the ultimate sports car complete with exceptional handling, high-end leather, wood finishes, and "craftsmanship," but it probably doesn't spend all that much more than Lincoln does. Lincolns are also luxury cars and, like Porsche, in 2016 Lincoln did not offer any new vehicles with manufacturer suggested retail price (MSRP) below $30,000. But Lincoln did have three vehicles with starting MSRP below $40,000. Porsche did not. If you wanted to own a new Porsche in 2016, you had pay at least $47,000, and the maker of luxury racing vehicles only offers one option at that level. Porsche is certainly offering performance, but exclusivity is well established by virtue of price. High MSRP is contributing to the intangible exclusive image that Porsche customers value in the brand.

Differentiation strategy is at play with all luxury goods and services, but the application of differentiation is not limited to high-end products. Chick-fil-A uses differentiation in the fast-food market by offering exceptional customer experiences. AT&T distinguishes itself among wireless carriers with its U-verse bundle of cellular, internet, and TV services, allowing customers to pay one bill and enjoy lower prices as a reward for loyalty. Hyundai offers extensive warranties to differentiate its line of affordable vehicles from competitors. Differentiation can be accomplished many ways, all of which affect perceived value. Typically, if you're focusing on differentiation, you're going to be thinking about things like product features and customer service and enabling differentiation in those areas of your business. You might choose to add a feature to your product or service to enhance perceived value. Ideally, you can find a way to do so without a significant increase in cost of production or service delivery. Amazon Prime is a paid service available to Amazon customers that gains shoppers access to a library of on-demand movies. But perhaps the biggest selling point or feature of the annual subscription is free two-day shipping on qualifying Amazon purchases. The perceived value to customers is high because customers get their goods delivered to their doorsteps in short order. As a bonus to Amazon, the same free service engenders customer loyalty. Amazon invests significant resources to ensure its superior supply-chain management enables consistent two-day delivery of goods to loyal Prime customers. If you're pursuing a differentiation strategy, you need to ask yourself what features you're offering and could offer to distinguish yourself in the marketplace, and what enabling resources and capabilities you might need to have in place to ensure you can deliver on promised features.

Customer service is another potential differentiator that can go a long way to earning and keeping a competitive advantage in the marketplace. Chick-fil-A's award-winning customer service enables the relatively small chain to outperform all other quick-service restaurants in per-unit sales. In 2015, the chicken chain averaged $3.9 million in per-unit sales. Jason's Deli came in at a distant second with $2.6 million. McDonald's ranked fifth in per-unit sales with $2.5 million.[25] Service can really make a difference. This is equally true for consultants, professional service providers, and trade services, whether consumer focused or business-to-business. If customers perceive that they are well served, they tend to come back. If customers are truly impressed with service, they are likely to tell others and refer new customers. An investment in enabling capabilities such as a friendly receptionist to handle calls and build customer relationships can be a valuable differentiator. How might customer service differentiate you from your competition? Are there enabling resources and capabilities you need to put in place to ensure your customer service adds value?

 You need to consider both cost and differentiation if you want to be competitive.

Whether you're working to enable a primarily cost leadership or primarily differentiation strategy, there are enabling resources and capabilities that you will need to put in place to defend against erosion of distinctive competencies and to make your strategy work. But always keep in mind that these are just two general approaches to doing business and that you need to consider both cost and differentiation if you want to be competitive. You may also need to consider digging a bit deeper into other aspects of management strategy, particularly if you are looking at operating multiple businesses or working internationally. Without a doubt, you need to consider some of the basics of any organizational operation. You very likely need enablers related to things like accounting, human resource management, and finance. Since these are enablers, they need not be your strengths, but you should educate yourself and perhaps find a partner or partners that can specialize in areas that might not be your area of expertise. Should you sense that you need more information on any of the topics associated with enabling factors, such as operational strategy, do seek it out. Many business schools offer executive and continuing education courses. You might choose to seek out other books on specific topics. However you approach it, educating yourself is always a good idea. Whatever you do, do not ignore these areas of your operation. Instead, prioritize.

Prioritizing Key Enablers

I've covered a lot of ground in this chapter. That's because there is a lot of your business operation wrapped up in enabling factors. These are, in fact, the things that enable you to do business and create value in the marketplace, so there is a lot to be considered here. But we must be realistic. You cannot do it all. You need to focus on enabling those resources and capabilities most critical to your value creation and rareness. I developed the Enablers Matrix to help you identify the enabling factors most critical to your operation and establish priorities accordingly. The Enablers Matrix picks up where we left off with the Erosion Matrix. As you can see in Figure 7: Enablers Matrix for Competencies, the tool references previously considered eroding factors, prompting you to list out distinctive competencies and those associated eroding factors with the highest erosion ratings. Having brought this information over from the Erosion Matrix for Competencies, you use the Enablers Matrix for Competencies to list possible enablers for each eroding factor. From there, you will consider general enablers not associated with distinctive competencies but necessary for operations. You're developing an inventory of enablers, and once you've done that, you'll prioritize them. A blank version of the matrix is available in the Resources section in the back of the book and online at ThinkBeyondValue.com.

ENABLERS MATRIX FOR COMPETENCIES

DISTINCTIVE COMPETENCY ⊕	ERODING FACTOR ⊖ List those with the highest erosion ratings	ENABLING FACTOR List as many enabling factors as you can think of that may work against each eroding factor	FREQUENCY OF NEED Scale of 1–10, with 1 being rarely and 10 being daily	IMPACT OF NOT HAVING ENABLER Scale of 1–10, with 10 being a profound negative impact on the organization	ENABLING SCORE Frequency multiplied by impact

GENERAL OPERATIONAL ENABLERS
1. List all operational enablers you can think of 2. Rate frequency, impact and calculate enabling score

GENERAL ENABLERS OF COMPETENCIES ⊕			FREQUENCY OF NEED Scale of 1–10, 1 being rarely and 10 being daily	IMPACT OF ENABLER ⊕ Scale of 1–10, with 10 being a profound positive impact	ENABLING SCORE Frequency multiplied by impact

Figure 7: Enablers Matrix for Competencies

At this point in the V-REEL Framework, you're really getting into the substance of your strategy building. You very likely have a lot of information in your head or scattered across notepads and whiteboards.

The Enablers Matrix for Competencies will help you organize all of that and provide the beginning of a plan forward. So hang with me here. It is worth the effort. I'll walk through each section to get you started.

You'll notice that there are two sections of the matrix. Beginning in the top section, you'll capture eroding factors with the highest erosion ratings as calculated in your Erosion Matrix for Competencies. To begin, list both the distinctive competencies and the highest rated eroding factors using the first two columns of the matrix. This will give you an inventory at a glance of what you need to be considering. Having done that, you'll list enablers that defend against each eroding factor. You may have multiple enablers for any given eroding factor. For each enabling factor you list, work across the row, rating frequency of need and the impact of *not* having that enabler in place. Remember, when considering distinctive competencies, enablers defend against eroding factors. Sometimes the consequences of not having those enablers can be devastating. Other times, an enabler may not be all that impactful. So, rate the impact of not having the enabler in place on a scale of one to ten, with ten indicating a profound negative impact. Once you've input frequency and impact ratings for each enabler, you can simply multiply frequency times impact to calculate an enabling score for each enabling factor. With those calculations done, you can see which enablers have the highest rating, indicating they are most important to your value creation. Ask yourself if you can implement those enablers with the highest enabling scores. If not, either work on identifying additional enablers or cycle back through value and rareness to identify distinctive competencies you can better defend against erosion. If, on the other hand, you do feel confident that you can put the highest scoring enablers in place, you're ready to work with the bottom half of your Enablers Matrix for Competencies considering general operational enablers.

Using the bottom half of the matrix, you'll list those general operational enablers you need to run your organization. Things like office space, a point of sale system, accounting capability, payroll systems, and human resource management might be among the general enablers you need to operate. The idea here is to think about what you need to get business done that isn't already addressed above. List those things here. Once again, you'll rate frequency of need and the impact of the enabler. Note that when rating the impact of these general operational enablers, you are rating the impact of having the enabler in place. Impact can range from (1) little or no positive impact to (10) a profound positive impact. Finally, you calculate enabler ratings by multiplying frequency by impact. Stepping back and looking at your entire Enablers Matrix for Competencies, you will see that some enablers score higher than others, indicating a higher priority for your operations. This gives you a clear picture of the enablers you need to put in place to defend distinctive competencies against erosion and manage your operations.

By thinking through enabling factors, establishing priorities, and considering topics in more depth as needed, you will strengthen your overall strategy and gain a more complete picture of the various resources and capabilities required for your operation. As you do so, you may start to wonder how long your distinctive competencies will remain distinctive. You're aware that competitors are likely to try replicating your success. You know erosion is going to set in at some point. So how long do you have? That is the question we consider with the *L* in V-REEL. We will explore longevity and its implications for value creation in Chapter 5.

Case Study: The Walmart Way— Establishing and Enabling Strategy Early and Often

In the early 1960s, three different retailers entered the market as price leaders in the big-box department store market. Kmart opened its first store in Garden City, Michigan outside Detroit, and the first Target store opened in a suburb outside Saint Paul, Minnesota. Both positioned themselves in the suburbs to serve the large numbers of families that continued to move away from city centers to bedroom communities. Sam Walton also opened his first Walmart store in the early 60s, but he did two things from the very start of the company that would shape its competitive advantage for years to come. First, Walmart didn't compete head-to-head with Target and Kmart—not at first, anyway. Instead, the first Walmart stores were established in smaller towns away from big metropolitan areas. Walton was using geography to work in his favor. He opened stores in communities with populations less than five thousand. No big-box competitors were interested in such small markets, enabling Walton to position Walmart stores as the place to shop in smaller communities. Second, Walton committed to offering the lowest prices. He believed that by lowering his profit margins he would attract more customers and ultimately earn more through high sales volume.

Walton's theory proved true. In just five years, Walmart grew to twenty-four locations with $12.7 million in sales.[26] By the time the company turned ten, it was listed on the New York Stock Exchange, had grown to fifty-one stores, and recorded $78 million in sales.[27] It was 1972 and Walmart was just getting started. By the 1980s, Walmart became the fastest company at the time to reach $1 billion in annual sales.[28] It had 276 stores. What enabled such fantastic growth? How did Walton do it? Walton, from the very beginning, knew he would pursue a cost leadership strategy in the retail market and remained laser focused on that strategy to generate high-volume sales. With high sales volume, economies of scale became an enabling factor for keeping costs low. The large stores could offer a wide variety of merchandise, handle larger volumes of inventory, and operate more efficiently than smaller competitors. And as the company grew, the benefits of scale grew with it: Walmart enjoyed increasing buying power as it expanded, yet another enabler for lowering costs.

Of course, keeping costs low was key. With expansion of stores and supplies came the need for efficient supply chain management and logistics. Walmart anticipated that the value of the investment in supply chain systems would far outweigh costs. By 1983, the company was leading the industry in technology innovation. It replaced cash registers with computerized point-of-sale systems that worked with product barcodes to enable inventory management.[29] In 1987, Walmart launched the largest private satellite communication system at the time, enabling communications with suppliers and ensuring the products customers wanted were available when they wanted them.[30] To further enable its cost leadership strategy, Walmart located distribution centers within 130 miles of the stores and ran its own trucking fleet employing experienced drivers, lowering costs. By 1989, its distribution costs were 1.7 percent of its sales.[31] That was less than half of K-Mart's costs at the time and less than a third of what Sears was spending.[32]

Logistics and supply chain management, which initially were enablers of the low-cost strategy, became distinctive competencies that served Walmart well. Today, the company is the largest private employer in the world,[33] with more than eleven thousand stores worldwide. Still, its information systems and logistics capabilities are tangible and observable. Competitors can buy the same computer systems and link systems with suppliers just like Walmart. As time passed, Walmart gradually lost the degree of advantage—of distinctive competency—that it had during previous decades because companies like Target and others became increasingly efficient as well. The eroding factor for Walmart has been replication; the others are behind Walmart, but they can do the same things Walmart has done.

Today, Walmart may be in danger of falling from parity. It struggles to have distinctive competencies and to keep ahead of competitors like Target and, increasingly, Amazon. In response to Amazon's burgeoning online retail, Walmart is investing considerably in its online shopping experience and introducing customer-focused services like curbside pick-up of online grocery orders, all the while working to build up enablers to ensure that it remains focused on cost leadership in a changing retail marketplace.

Key Steps and Useful Tools for Identifying Enablers

1. BEGIN WITH YOUR EROSION MATRIX, FOCUSING ON ITEMS WITH THE HIGHEST EROSION RATING.

2. LIST ENABLING FACTORS TO DEFEND AGAINST EACH OF THE ERODING FACTORS WITH THE HIGHEST RATINGS.

    A. IF YOU CAN IDENTIFY WORKABLE ENABLERS AGAINST EROSION, MOVE ON TO STEP 3 BELOW.

    B. IF YOU ARE NOT ABLE TO IDENTIFY VIABLE ENABLERS TO DEFEND AGAINST ERODING FACTORS, RETURN TO VALUE AND RARENESS TO IDENTIFY OTHER POTENTIAL DISTINCTIVE COMPETENCIES.

3. IDENTIFY OPERATIONAL ENABLERS.

    A. CONSIDER YOUR GENERAL BUSINESS STRATEGY (COST LEADERSHIP OR DIFFERENTIATION).

    B. SEEK OUT ADDITIONAL INFORMATION AS NEEDED TO EDUCATE YOURSELF ON TOPICS SUCH AS BUSINESS-LEVEL STRATEGY, CORPORATE-LEVEL STRATEGY, ACCOUNTING, FINANCE, AND HUMAN RESOURCE MANAGEMENT.

    C. LIST ADDITIONAL ENABLERS NEEDED TO SUPPORT YOUR GENERAL OPERATIONS.

4. PRIORITIZE—USE THE ENABLERS MATRIX FOR COMPETENCIES.

    A. INVENTORY ALL IDENTIFIED ENABLERS BY LISTING THEM IN THE ENABLERS MATRIX.

    B. RATE THE FREQUENCY AND IMPACT OF EACH ENABLER AND CALCULATE THE ENABLING SCORE.

    C. ENABLERS WITH THE HIGHEST ENABLING SCORES SHOULD RECEIVE HIGHEST PRIORITY.

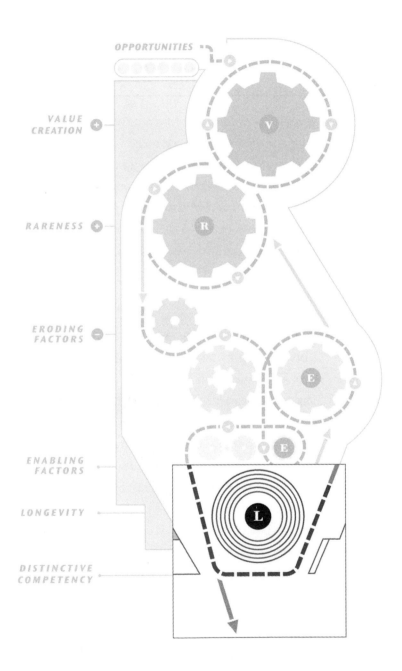

OPPORTUNITIES

VALUE
CREATION

RARENESS

ERODING
FACTORS

ENABLING
FACTORS

LONGEVITY

DISTINCTIVE
COMPETENCY

CHAPTER 5

Time Will Tell, but Consider It Anyway

Remember when you were hunting for distinctive competencies? You were exploring your external and internal environments, trying to find those valuable and rare resources and capabilities that might push you ahead of the competition. You didn't do all that work for a few moments of glory. You did it because you want something special that you can sustain over time by protecting against erosion with enabling resources and capabilities. The holy grail of strategic management is a sustainable competitive advantage—the ability to outperform the competition and earn a profit for a sustained period. Sustainability requires you to look ahead and try to understand what the future holds. Some might do that very naturally when considering erosion because you are asking what will erode your distinctive competencies. Can you really ask that question without also asking when erosion might set in? Well, you can… but you shouldn't.

As you consider the *L* in V-REEL, the whole idea is to recognize that the world is a dynamic place—and try to understand how long you have before things change. Up to now, you've been considering and trying to understand your situation as it exists today. But if you have an awesome set of distinctive competencies that you've protected against erosion with enabling resources and capabilities, you must ask yourself these questions: How long do I have before things change? How long will this good thing last? How long before I need something new in place so I can continue to create value? Big, publicly traded corporations like IBM understand well the need to consider longevity. They must understand it well because shareholders expect returns, and good returns come when you outperform the competition and continue to find ways to do so over time. IBM and any other company that has been around for any real length of time has had some degree of success considering longevity. But even if you don't have shareholders or a board looking over your shoulder, you want to compete well. Not just today, but into the future.

 If you want to be in business tomorrow, you need to think what tomorrow might look like.

If you want to be in business tomorrow, you need to think what tomorrow might look like. And if you want to be in business next year or ten years from now, you need to think about what the world might look like next year and a decade from now. And that's why we have the *L* in V-REEL. We want to make sure that we are looking ahead to the future and preparing for what it may hold. In doing so, we may identify more eroding factors that we need to address, or we may uncover new opportunities to form distinctive competencies. We could even discover that our big idea isn't so great after all because eroding factors are coming on too fast, and there just isn't enough time to build up enabling resources and capabilities to defend against erosion.

The point is, the future has a lot to tell us, so we need to look ahead and try to understand what that is. Yes, I know, we actually cannot *know* what the future holds. But you cannot use uncertainty as an excuse not to pay attention to what's going on in the world around you and make an educated guess. This deep into the V-REEL Framework, you're not just making stuff up. You know your market because you've studied your external environment. You know your organization because you've taken the time to look inside and understand your situation. And given these things, you're able to make some educated guesses about what might change and, equally important, when changes might occur. So you make some predictions, and based on those predictions you prepare for what may come, all with the hope of extending the life of your distinctive competencies as long as possible.

In this chapter, we will look at why it really is worthwhile to make some guesses about the future, even if you guess poorly. We will explore how to get an understanding of the longevity of your situation, and we will look at some organizations that have achieved longevity in hopes of learning from their successes. Let's jump in and begin considering the future. Only there can we hope to uncover the secrets to longevity.

The Case for Guesswork

Yogi Berra said it well: "It's tough to make predictions, especially about the future."[34] Exactly. So why bother? Obviously, we don't know what tomorrow will bring, and that is part of the reason most people avoid thinking about this issue of the future. It's hard, and it is imperfect.

Even I could make the case that it's kind of silly to try to predict the future when you know you are likely to predict poorly. But you must think about the future and guess what it may bring even though you know you're probably going to get it wrong. It's like life in general. You know you should plan ahead. That's what strategy is all about, both at the personal level and organizationally. If you're not thinking ahead and not thinking in terms of how long these present conditions will hold, you're doing yourself a disservice. So yes, I am talking about doing something that is inherently imperfect. It is difficult, perhaps even impossible, to come up with any predictions in which you are absolutely confident. But you do it anyway because you need something—some assumption—upon which to base your decisions. Still, you always know that you're very likely to get it wrong. It's okay. You're in good company.

I watch a lot of interviews on RealVision TV where people who are macro-investors and macro-analysts think and talk about the world they see around them and what the future will hold and then make investments accordingly. During the interviews, there is a lot of talk about what's happening in politics and in various markets around the world. Based on all this discussion, the people who are interviewed—some of whom are managing billions of dollars—are making predictions about the future. And every one of them essentially says the same thing about their predictions. Basically, they say that they probably have it all wrong. Or sometimes they use a different caveat. They'll say that some event is certain to happen eventually, but there is no way to accurately predict when. In both cases, these investors and analysts are acknowledging very candidly that they are very likely wrong in some respect. Still, they keep making predictions. And so should you.

Even though your predictions will likely be wrong, the exercise of making them will leave you better prepared for an always uncertain future. You can learn from your mistakes. You can get better at thinking about the future. Business leaders and strategists may very naturally think about longevity, but they often fail to intentionally consider the future. That leaves them vulnerable and unprepared for what may come.

 Even though your predictions will likely be wrong, the exercise of making them will leave you better prepared for an always uncertain future.

This process of going through V-REEL should leave you informed and more prepared. You've thought about how your organization creates value and the resources and capabilities you have. You understand your distinctive competencies, what might erode them away, and what you need to have to enable them to create value. Finally, you are prepared to consider longevity. How long will the conditions in which you are operating today hold? How long until things start changing? This is the longevity question. The answer provides the final reality check you need. You must know if the big idea you've worked so hard to build up and protect might have some potential to work long enough to create a competitive advantage in the marketplace.

Asking the Longevity Question

Everything has a shelf life. Canned goods don't last forever. Medicines expire. Fashions change. And your big idea will lose its luster. It just will. But if you make an effort to understand when your idea might expire, you can either prepare for that eventuality by bringing along a new idea for value creation, or you might be able to extend the life of your original idea. But first, you need to know what you're dealing with. You need to know how long you have before your rare and valuable idea fades into the ordinary and becomes obsolete or otherwise erodes away. In business for more than one hundred years, IBM has had more than one of its product lines become obsolete. The IBM Selectric typewriter introduced in 1961[35] was the first in a line of innovative typewriters and word processors that provided IBM a competitive advantage in the business market for nearly a generation. But by the 1980s, others had caught up to IBM's word processing capability. IBM was prepared with a whole new offering, debuting the first IBM personal computer in 1981.[36] But any first-to-market advantage Big Blue enjoyed didn't last long. By 1995, IBM clones flooded the market and the company had to go in a totally new direction. Clearly, IBM made the transition, but how? How did it anticipate that the shift was needed? And how can you? How do you figure out how long you have before erosion takes its toll?

When considering longevity, you're looking at the total picture of your organization—your internal and external environments—and trying to assess how long the current conditions are likely to last. When you were identifying eroding factors and enablers, you were asking what might happen and what you might do about it. When thinking in terms of longevity, your focus shifts to ask when those same factors might come into play. And you also want to know if by taking this action or that one, how might the current conditions change? And how might that change affect the amount of time you have? *How long?* That's the longevity question and you need to ask it often.

 When considering longevity, you're looking at the total picture of your organization—your internal and external environments—and trying to assess how long the current conditions are likely to last.

In thinking about longevity, you're not only looking at the eroding factors and asking how long before they set in. You're looking at the entire picture of your organization and asking questions: How long before things change inside the organization? How about in the external environment? How long will it take to establish the enablers needed to keep erosion under control? You ask all these questions to form some assumptions with some degree of confidence; you ask questions to understand how much time you have under the current conditions. That's the time you have to prepare for change.

Take a restaurant, for example. Say the restaurant has brand-new recipes. They've tested well and are suited to target demographics. The restaurant owners have done their research and know the consumer response to their new menu. They hired the right talent—managers and such—so the enabling factors are in place. Now they consider longevity. They ask the longevity questions: If I open this restaurant and it's a hit, how long will it be before the eroding factors set in as competitors try to imitate what I'm doing? How long before the owners burn out from running the restaurant? Considering these and other questions, they decide they have about three years before they're going to need to do something different. The "something different" might be selling or perhaps opening a new restaurant with a different concept. Or maybe it's franchising. It could be any number of things, but three years from now the restaurant owners need to be prepared to make a change. The restaurant owners established a timeline by looking at the current conditions and thinking about how long they will hold. They realized they've got about a three-year window with the current set of circumstances. And given current conditions and what they see coming at them, the business makes sense. But at the end of three years they've got to make some kind of move to continue creating value.

As you've been thinking through erosion and enabling factors you probably had at least some sense of the need to ask the longevity question. How long until the eroding factors at the top of your list walk through your door? Realistically, how long have you got to get things in place and enjoy good returns? How long before you need to start making changes? In the restaurant example, there is a window of three years and that seems reasonable. You can work with three years. But as you look at your situation and ask how long you have, it is possible you will realize that you don't have any time at all. You might see that nothing you have is going to last for more than a hiccup and a half. That's not long enough to create any real value. If you realize you don't have enough time, you may also realize moving forward isn't the best idea. And that's okay. Even this deep in the V-REEL Framework, you need to be willing to let an idea go, and you should do so happily. It is really good to recognize that the shelf life of your idea simply isn't long enough to justify the investment. Being aware of that before you put all your resources into something or ask your leadership or investors to do so—that is nothing short of a gift. We consider longevity so we can make some educated guesses, form assumptions about our situation, and answer the longevity questions; we do all this so that we can either move forward with confidence or walk away with confidence.

By considering longevity, you are not just better prepared for the future and better prepared to handle what might come at you. You are more aware of how near or far eroding factors are or how much time you need to build up enablers. Awareness informs your decision making. It allows you to be intentional and decide to go forward on your current path or stop and choose another.

Time as a Factor in Priorities

If you did not naturally move to considerations of time when you were thinking about erosion and enabling factors, the L in V-REEL will help you get there. In fact, longevity can and should inform your priorities. Think back through the framework and consider value and rareness and those distinctive competencies you identified. How long will they last? Think about the eroding factors you identified with high erosion ratings. How long before the erosion becomes an issue? Enabling factors—how long will it take to get them in place? And once you do, how will that affect longevity? You've done a lot of the work identifying the "what." When talking about longevity, you are considering the "when" and acknowledging that you're operating in a dynamic environment where circumstances will change. By keeping that in mind and making some well-informed predictions about how and when changes might occur, you're preparing yourself to be nimble. But if you just go forward and operate based on your understanding of the situation as it exists today, something is going to come along that changes things. And it could be a real problem. It's like you're on a path, and you know what the path is because you planned and researched. It's a good path, so you're going down it. Meanwhile, someone out in front of you and someone else behind you is putting down rails, and suddenly there is a track; it is no longer just a great path. It's a rail line and a train is headed right at you. If that happens, it is very likely you didn't really consider longevity.

If, on the other hand, you recognize that you're operating in a dynamic environment where change is a constant, then you pay attention to what's happening around you and you adjust accordingly. You make the decision to get off the path, or hop on the train and somehow add value. Whatever the case, your consideration of longevity provided the opportunity to choose how to respond to the environment rather than become a victim of it. Because you consider the longevity of your situation, you might be able to affect it, extending the life of your distinctive competencies or creating new ones all together.

Recall Blockbuster's Antioco. He acknowledged that his environment was changing and set out to leverage his relationship with movie houses to bundle content with cable providers under the Blockbuster brand. Meanwhile, he began using the internet to launch the company's All Access program, answering the fledgling Netflix mail order subscription service by providing the company's considerable customer base with the ability to order their entertainment online, receive it in the mail, and even return it to stores. Antioco understood that he was in the business of entertainment and that the Internet was changing how entertainment would be delivered. In response, he began building up capabilities that would leverage his existing resources—a sizeable customer base and relationships with film studios—to ensure Blockbuster could continue to lead in the home-movie entertainment space despite changes in the external environment. Of course, we all know the fate of Blockbuster. Judging by the company's growing presence in online entertainment at the time of Antioco's departure, it does not seem that his sense of timing in the marketplace can be blamed for the company's downfall.

Getting the timing right is certainly helpful, but I don't buy the notion that timing is everything. The exercise of thinking about how your situation will change over time is far more important than getting the timing just right. There are people out there who try to do forecasts, and you can look up forecasting information relevant to your industry, but you must make a judgement call. You're making some guesses, so it is not about getting caught up in specific timeframes. If you can say with confidence that something is going to happen in six months, great! But that's not really necessary. What we are doing here is prioritizing. We can look at the various factors we are facing in the future and say this thing is more likely to happen sooner than this other thing. We can then pay more attention to the more immediate concern. Or we see the impact of this thing is very significant, and it is coming up quickly. It is the higher priority. I'm not looking for specificity on a timeline—although that's great if you can get it—I'm looking more for how to prioritize. What do I need to be doing first, second, third? Allow the question of time to inform priorities.

Time has become a factor for major players in the food industry that have been responding to changing consumer preferences in recent years—

to the tune of billions of dollars in mergers and acquisitions. Giants like Hormel and General Mills recognized that they needed to be in the natural food space if they were to remain relevant in the marketplace. They have spent hundreds of millions of dollars to acquire once-niche players Annie's, Inc. and Applewood Farms.[37] Consumer demand for organic and non-GMO products was eroding profits among traditional food suppliers, so major players in the food industry had to respond or risk losing the ability to compete. Time became a more serious factor as soon as the first major player in the industry made an acquisition to enter the natural foods space. Priorities shifted accordingly, and an explosion of food industry mergers and acquisitions led to $116 billion in U.S. food industry deals in 2015[38] alone.

Just as major food industry players scanned the market and adjusted priorities, you must routinely monitor your external and internal environments, eroding factors and enabling factors, and look at them with a longer view. You ask how long before things change and, with that additional consideration, adjust your expectations and priorities. The last stop in the V-REEL Framework is important. Considering longevity is something that you force yourself to stop and do because, given the context of everything that you've thought about, you need to grapple with what sort of bang for the buck you might expect to get over time. If you determine you have enough time to achieve some degree of distinctiveness in the marketplace, then you can get to work. Start building up distinctive competencies and defending against erosion. But that's not all. You should also spend just a little more time in the V-REEL Framework—this time considering *in*competencies.

At this stage, you've identified that you have some real distinctiveness in the marketplace, distinctiveness that you can defend and sustain—at least for a while. Given that great news, it's a good idea to consider incompetencies—those pesky things that, left unattended, could make a mess of all the great work you've done to build up a competitive position. So that's up next. Onward into the realm of incompetencies. We will find them and seek out ways to eliminate or minimize them so that your competitive position has the potential to last.

Case Study: Betting the Company— Lessons in Longevity from Big Blue

In 2011, IBM celebrated one hundred years[39] of innovation and joined the elite group of American businesses to celebrate a centennial. Clearly, Big Blue made a few good guesses over the years to achieve that sort of longevity in an industry that is perhaps best known for change. When IBM was formed in 1911, tabulating machines, time recorders, and scales were among the most advanced technologies used in business and government. IBM had them all. But from the very earliest days of the company, its leadership had a keen sense of both its external and internal environments and—more importantly—time.

The first two decades of the twentieth century brought some of the most important technological advancements of our time. Einstein's theory of relativity and De Forest's triode vacuum tube would change the world, and IBM would be there to help the process along. Already leading in the early computing industry with big government contracts for census counting, IBM was well positioned to sell big contracts to solve complex problems. As technology advanced, IBM leaders—and Thomas J. Watson in particular—recognized that the key enabler to remain relevant and even lead in technology was a well-educated workforce that could use available technologies and invent new ones to solve customers' biggest problems. By 1916, Watson had established the company's employee education program and the famous "Think" slogan that is still in use today.[40]

By the 1920s, Watson's investment in employee education was paying off. IBMers, as employees came to be known, were expanding the company's product line with groundbreaking engineering. The IBM school time-control system, printing tabulator, and electric key punch brought the company to $19 million in gross income by 1930.[41] But with more than six thousand employees, the depression would bring a new challenge that no amount of technology could overcome. While other companies were reducing their workforces to try to survive the depression, Watson hired additional staff and continued to invest in education throughout the economic crisis.[42] Watson was maintaining the long view and building a distinctive competency that would position him to lead when the market recovered. It was an enormous gamble. IBM factories ran for six years—with no buying customers—producing a huge inventory of tabulating equipment and straining the company's resources. But the risk paid off. When the Social Security Act of 1935 required the biggest accounting operation of all time, IBM was the only bidder that could quickly provide the necessary equipment to maintain employment records for twenty-six million people. That success led to more government contracts, and by 1940, propelled the company to $45 million in gross income with more than twelve thousand employees.[43]

By 1956, IBM had become an international leader in data processing and supercomputing, but Big Blue was facing an eroding factor of massive proportions. Its entire existing computer product line—comprising more than 70 percent of the company—was facing obsolescence. Customers needed more memory, and none of its existing computers had the capacity. IBM's research and development team presented a plan to IBM leadership that would replace all the company's existing computer lines and revolutionize computing in the process. Fortune magazine called it IBM's $5 billion gamble.[44] This time it was Thomas Watson, Jr. who bet the company, and once again, the bet paid off. The IBM System/360 line was the first general-purpose computer product line that used the same basic machine and configured it for different applications. The company enjoyed decades of success with the System/360 line. So much so that through the 1970s, more than 70 percent of mainframes sold were IBM's, and by 1982, more than half of IBM's revenue came from descendants of the System/360.[45]

Despite the System/360 success, IBM leaders knew they needed to continue to innovate or risk obsolescence. Retired System/360 project director Fred Brooks said it well in an interview reflecting on the company's first one hundred years: "You've got to stay alert and you've got to be nimble on your feet and you've got to recognize that what was true yesterday will not be true tomorrow in terms of technology and what you can do with it."[46]

Mr. Brooks is right, of course. Despite IBM's leading position in computing technology, replication and even substitution became eroding factors. The company missed some key technology shifts and went from Wall Street winner in 1984 to posting an $8 billion loss just ten years later.[47] IBM was forced to reinvent itself once again. When Louis Gerstner took the reins in 1993, he returned the company's focus to its fundamental ability to solve customer problems. To ensure that IBM could do that on a large scale, Gerstner reversed plans to break apart the company.[48] He understood that IBM's collective technology expertise and array of business activities combined synergistically to form a competency bundle this is rare and valuable to corporate and government customers. He recognized the distinctive competency bundle and that breaking up the components would, over time, erode the company's ability to create value. He took steps to stop the erosion, and today IBM is largely a professional services company.

Still, innovation is a significant part of IBM's identity and central to its ability to solve complex problems and, of course, remain relevant.

In 2012 the company filed the most US patents for the twentieth consecutive year.[49] Clearly, IBM has no intention of getting out of the business of innovation. Today, Big Blue's big gamble is on cognitive computing. CEO Virginia Rometty presented the big new idea with a simple phrase that harkens back to the earliest days of IBM: Outthink. This simple phrase is introducing the world to what Rometty is calling a new era—the cognitive era. And change is happening fast. IBM claims that more advancements were made in just two years of IBM's Watson cognitive platform than in the past ten years with existing technologies.[50] Clearly, time continues to be a factor. Did IBM give itself enough lead time with Watson? How long before competition comes along to erode the distinctive competency IBM is building around Watson? Time will tell, of course, but without a doubt, IBM is asking the time questions. And based on IBM's best guesses, one of the foremost companies in the world is making some very large gambles on the future.

Key Steps in Considering Longevity

1. REVIEW WHAT YOU KNOW:
   A. SCAN YOUR EXTERNAL ENVIRONMENT.
   B. SCAN YOUR INTERNAL ENVIRONMENT.
2. ASK THE LONGEVITY QUESTIONS:
   A. HOW LONG BEFORE THE EXTERNAL ENVIRONMENT CHANGES?
   B. HOW LONG BEFORE THINGS CHANGE IN THE INTERNAL ENVIRONMENT?
3. REVISIT ERODING AND ENABLING FACTORS AND ASK:
   A. HOW LONG BEFORE EROSION SETS IN?
      I. CAN YOU DO ANYTHING ABOUT IT?
      II. IF SO, HOW DOES THAT AFFECT YOUR LONGEVITY?
   B. HOW LONG BEFORE YOU CAN PUT ENABLING RESOURCES IN PLACE?
      I. CAN YOU GET THEM IN PLACE SOON ENOUGH?
      II. IF SO, HOW DOES THAT AFFECT LONGEVITY?
4. CONSIDER THE WHOLE PICTURE AND ASK:
   A. WHAT PRIORITIES NEED TO BE ADJUSTED GIVEN YOUR RESPONSES TO THE LONGEVITY QUESTIONS?
   B. DO YOU HAVE ENOUGH TIME?
5. GIVEN YOUR ANSWERS TO THE LONGEVITY QUESTIONS, PRIORITIZE.
   A. WHAT DO YOU NEED TO DO FIRST?
   B. WHAT DO YOU NEED TO DO SECOND?
   C. AND SO ON…

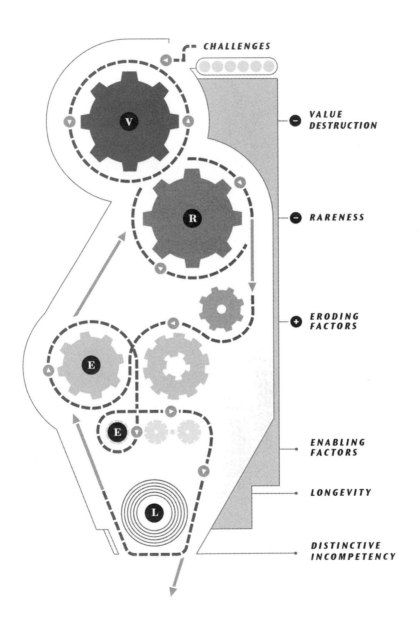

CHALLENGES

VALUE
DESTRUCTION

RARENESS

ERODING
FACTORS

ENABLING
FACTORS

LONGEVITY

DISTINCTIVE
INCOMPETENCY

CHAPTER 6

On the Flip Slide

U p to this point in our strategy discussions, I've been focusing on value creation. I've talked about distinctive competencies and all the things you can do to preserve them over time. That's generally an enjoyable exercise. After all, you're thinking about how you might make something and put it out there for the world. That's all good. It's exciting! But it's not the whole story. You need to work through one final set of considerations before you can call your strategy formulation process "complete." You need to consider *in*competencies. These are the value-destroying menaces lurking about in your organization that could very well be tearing down the value creation you've worked hard to protect and extend. I admit, it is much more fun to focus on creating value and doing something people are going to pay for. It is much more enjoyable to do that than to talk about what might be going on in your organization that might be destroying value. But you must deal with reality.

Realistically, if you're lucky, you have some really great positives working for you—strong distinctive competencies that are well-defended against erosion for the long haul. But if you have really strong negatives that go unaddressed, no amount of enabling factors will save you. Incompetencies can kill your really great positives. You need to think in terms of incompetencies as well as competencies. Because you've already worked through the V-REEL Framework, you're familiar with it, so this time through is generally quicker. You've done much of the research and thinking about your internal and external environments already. You just need to step back through the framework and turn the conversation around. This time, instead of talking about how you might create value, the entire discussion is about how you might be destroying value.

As you look around for destructive forces, you will again seek out rareness, but this time rareness is not such a good thing. You will identify eroding factors and find that erosion of incompetencies is actually something you want to encourage. You will work your way through V-REEL asking questions:

- Where am I destroying value?
- Where am I doing things where one plus one is still one—or less than one?
- Is there any anti-synergy?
- Do I break more than I make?
- Where do those things happen? How? Why?

Incompetencies are the value-destroying menaces lurking about in your organization that could very well be tearing down the value creation you've worked hard to protect and extend.

We ask these questions because we all have incompetencies—in our personal lives and our organizations. We all do some things less effectively than they could be done. We work to identify those incompetencies and then try to understand if they are common among our peers or if they are distinctive to us. If your shortcomings are rare in your marketplace, that could be a real problem. The incompetency could potentially offset any competencies that you have (1 + -1 = 0). That's why you must ask yourself how rare an incompetency is. If I were playing basketball and everybody else was 5'9" like me, great! But as soon as somebody shows up who is 6'7", we are all toast. So in playing basketball, I have a bit of an incompetency because of my height, but if everybody else I'm playing against is the same height, my average stature isn't a problem. But if I'm the only 5'9" guy and everybody else is 6'7", I have a truly distinctive incompetency in playing basketball.

That's the basic idea, here. You are trying to determine if you have any truly distinctive incompetencies. It's not that you don't want to get rid of other incompetencies; it's that you want to find the ones that have real potential to offset any distinctive competency you have. That's why you think about the rareness of incompetencies.

In this chapter, we will work our way through the entire V-REEL Framework with an eye on incompetencies. We'll discover when rareness isn't such a great thing and how erosion can work in your favor. We will identify where you might be enabling incompetency and consider how long you might need to break the habit. Let's get started on this somewhat less exciting—but ultimately very valuable—journey through V-REEL. Incompetencies, we are coming for you!

Uncovering Value Destruction

As you make the second pass though the V-REEL Framework, things might seem a bit topsy-turvy. When talking about incompetencies, rareness is actually bad. Erosion is good, and enablers could go either way. It may be a bit confusing at first. The incompetencies side of the framework is presented in Figure 8: The Flip Side of V-REEL—Uncovering Value Destruction. But you get the basic idea: incompetencies are inherently negative, and when you are the only kid on the court with the negative, that's pretty bad news. You really need to try to fix it. Eroding factors might be just what you need to kick that rare incompetency to the curb, because eroding away a bad thing is actually good! But before you can even think about erosion, you must know what needs to be eroded away. You return to the *V* in V-REEL with this question: How are we destroying value? You are taking stock of your situation based on what you've learned in the internal and external environments. You are asking a few more questions and keeping an open mind to see what these environments and the people around you can tell you about how you might be destroying value.

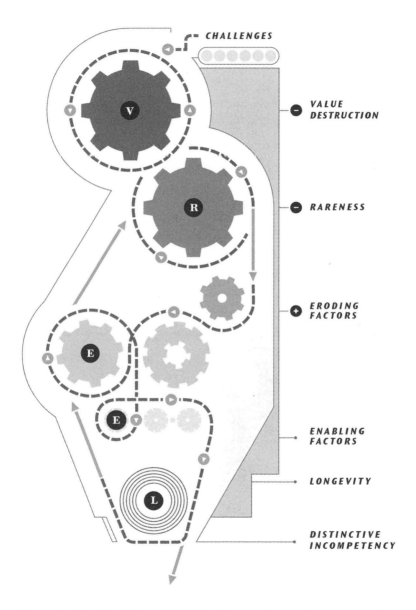

Figure 8: The Flip Side of V-REEL—Uncovering Value Destruction

As you start to search for incompetencies, it's useful to acknowledge that this topic may very well cause some anxiety, particularly if you're working with a team. It's tough enough to turn the microscope on yourself and honestly assess where things might need to change and to open your eyes to your own distinctive incompetencies. I think for most of us it is even more uncomfortable to turn a critical eye to our colleagues. And if you're an entrepreneur, you might find it still harder to look critically at your precious baby, but that baby is a business. And since it is so dear to you, it is a wise thing to step back and allow yourself to notice—in fact, to seek out—those places where things simply are not going as well as they could. You need to push past any anxiety and just get busy seeking out incompetencies. This isn't an invitation to be nasty, but it is a time for brutal honesty. Ask for brutally honest input from trusted friends and colleagues. They will very likely be valuable sources of insights as you move forward.

As you do move forward in search of incompetencies, keep in mind that in this pass through V-REEL, you are looking for *rare* incompetencies. Once again, we really need to consider value destruction and rareness in the same breath. It's just not practical—nor is it necessary—to address every little thing that isn't tip-top in the operation. As far as value destruction is concerned, the real danger exists when any incompetencies in your organization are rare among your peers. You consider rareness even as you are uncovering the incompetency, remaining in a sort of value-rareness loop as you work through your review of things. And just as you did when you were seeking out distinctive competencies, you will make note of any incompetencies that are both value destroying and rare.

When talking about incompetencies, rareness is actually bad. Erosion is good, and enablers could go either way.

That's what Steve Jobs did when he made his return to Apple in the late 1990s. The company was nearing bankruptcy. Clearly, something wasn't going well and Jobs recognized the incompetency. Apple products were no longer distinctive. Microsoft had introduced Windows and was distributing it broadly via low-cost personal computers. Meanwhile, Apple's offerings were well engineered but expensive and not very exciting. It had not developed a response to the competition. Essentially, Apple was a differentiator with no real distinctiveness. Jobs recognized the problem and had a vision to bring Apple back from prosaic to prominence. He would erode the incompetency with a combination of artful design, skillful marketing, and innovative user interfaces. Apple blazed a trail to a whole new market in mobile communications and computing.

Apple was in trouble, so it had to transform itself. But hopefully you can identify and address any distinctive incompetencies before things get desperate; you can seek out trouble spots and deal with them, preventing any real problems. So, what are incompetencies and where might you find them? In short, an incompetency is something that destroys value. Just like competencies, incompetencies can be from tangible or intangible sources. And they can be found at any level of your organization. It is an inefficiency, a lack of productivity, a mistake, or ineptness—anything that offsets your competencies. Sometimes incompetencies can be hard to find, but I think that many of them are fairly obvious if you start looking for them. Problems with faulty machinery or poor training are common areas of potential incompetency. But some can be sneaky. And by sneaky, I mean not overtly obvious when you start hunting for these things.

 To identify incompetencies be honest with yourself about what's not working.

Looking into the intangible realm, for instance, you may have formed a certain culture along with socially complex relationships within your organization, and that could all be great. But maybe you have somehow created some relationships that are not helpful and are destructive. Perhaps people withhold information from each other that they shouldn't. Or maybe people undermine each other, or people have contrary goals that don't serve your purpose. There could be a lot of subtle intangible stuff going on that is working against you. And if it is rare in your market, you may have a distinctive incompetency. It is easy to look at a piece of machinery and see that it doesn't work. Intangible things aren't always so easy. Maybe it's something that you have developed in terms of customer perception about you or your product. If customers have a bad experience that goes unresolved, that lingering impression can become an incompetency. These are aspects of your organization that might destroy value, and they could be tangible or intangible.

To identify incompetencies, you'll look back at your operations, invite team members to participate, seek insights from trusted friends and colleagues, and be honest with yourself about what's not working. Here are a few common incompetencies to spur your thinking about issues you might be facing:

- Aging and/or failing equipment
- An employee creating a toxic work environment

- Poor forecasting of costs and revenues
- Being held hostage by a key supplier
- A bad relationship with local city government
- Inventory control system isn't working—or doesn't exist
- Human resource policies are sub-par compared to competitors
- Your operations are in a place where minimum wage is higher than competitors
- Location is further away from customers than competitors
- Website and other marketing materials are outdated
- Competitors have patents and you don't
- Trademark lapsed
- Lack of focus or specialization
- Lack of strong vision or poor communication of strong vision to team

As you uncover incompetencies, you'll check your external environment and assess if this is a common issue or if you've got something rare and problematic that you need to address. The goal here is to identify value-destroying *and* rare resources and capabilities. Make note of them. Next, you will prioritize as you consider the restorative potential of eroding factors.

Putting Erosion to Work for Good

Having identified distinctive incompetencies that are working against your efforts to create value in the marketplace, create a new Erosion Matrix, this time to capture ways you might encourage erosion of any forces that are working against you. Looking at Figure 9: The Erosion Matrix for Incompetencies, you can see that it works much the same as the competencies matrix. The only difference is that the impact of erosion is positive, so eroding factors are good. Just as you did when you were considering erosion of competencies, you will list distinctive incompetencies and then consider any eroding factors you might put into place to address each one. Thus, eroding factors are directly tied to those identified distinctive incompetencies. If you've got a piece of machinery that is unreliable and destroying your ability to create value, then you might need to replace the machine, or perhaps you just need a new maintenance plan. If your incompetencies are more intangible, you might be dealing with a miss-match between key team members and the culture you are trying to establish, or negative customer perceptions. In these cases, the eroding factors might be a reorganization, perhaps even replacing the miss-matched team member, or enhancing customer relations.

EROSION MATRIX FOR INCOMPETENCIES

DISTINCTIVE INCOMPETENCY ⊖	ERODING FACTOR ⊕ To help overcome or defend against incompetency	LIKELIHOOD Scale of 1-10, with 10 being eroding factor currently exists or can easily be put in place	IMPACT Scale of 1-10, with 10 having profound and significant impact on the organization	EROSION RATING Likelihood multiplied by impact

Figure 9: The Erosion Matrix for Incompetencies

Whatever the case, it is important to identify distinctive incompetencies early and often and take corrective action to erode the damaging impacts. Walmart had to take corrective action against incompetencies when it began entering international markets. It went into markets assuming the models that had served its stores well in the U.S. would function well abroad, not recognizing that international variations in culture, local customs, and laws would dramatically affect the company's ability to create value as a low-cost leader. In some cases, Walmart had to go as far as completely pulling out of markets so it could take the time to put eroding factors into place to overcome major distinctive incompetencies. Walmart succeeded because it identified the incompetencies most destructive to its value creation and acted accordingly.

 It is important to identify distinctive incompetencies early and often and take corrective action to erode the damaging impacts.

The Erosion Matrix for Incompetencies will help you prioritize so you can focus efforts on those incompetencies most damaging to your value creation. Once you've identified eroding factors for each of your identified distinctive incompetencies, you're ready to begin rating each item in terms of likelihood and impact. In the case of incompetencies, first ask what is the likelihood that you can put the eroding factor in place? If you know you can get it done, or if the process is already in the works, then you'll give that factor a score of ten. But if the eroding factor you've identified is outside your control or unlikely for any reason, you'll give it a lower score. Next, you will score the potential impact of the eroding factor, assuming it is implemented, giving it a score between one and ten, with ten being a significant impact on the organization. Once you've scored each item, calculate the erosion rating. Those items with the highest score are the items with the highest potential for reducing the negative impacts of distinctive incompetencies. And those are the items on which you'll focus as you continue through the V-REEL Framework to consider enabling factors.

Enabling Damage Control

Having identified the distinctive incompetencies and eroding factors affecting your organization, you're ready to consider enabling factors. Like enabling factors of competencies, there are two kinds of enablers of *in*competencies. One type enables the eroding factors—and you want that. You want this type of enabler to help eroding factors get rid of the incompetency. The second type of enablers, general enablers, occur when you have some circumstance that directly enables or supports a distinctive incompetency. Clearly, that's not a good thing, so you need to try to eliminate the damaging enabling factor.

Beginning with enabling factors to support erosion of distinctive incompetencies, you can think about what resources and capabilities you might put into place that would encourage or even hasten the erosion of incompetencies. Basically, you're looking for ways to help erosion along. If your eroding factor is new equipment to replace the unreliable machinery at the root of your incompetency, then perhaps you need to enable that erosion with an infusion of capital. Or perhaps you need to acquire some new expertise to enable a stronger in-house training program so you can erode incompetencies in your business process. When Walmart pulled out of some international markets, it regrouped and put some key enablers in place to erode its incompetencies in each market. In many cases, Walmart's enablers in international markets took the form of acquisitions of existing companies that had a strong presence in the market, thus helping Walmart achieve a foothold while gaining much-needed local insight and credibility. As you can see, these enablers of erosion are not the eroding factors themselves. Instead, enablers are the additional resources and capabilities needed to hasten the elimination of incompetency.

Domino's Pizza was faced with a painful eroding factor in 2009 when it tied for last in a survey of consumer taste preferences.[51] Harsh consumer criticism revealed Domino's had, perhaps, pushed too far on logistics and delivery times, failing to notice as competitors upped their flavor games. A distinctive incompetency sneaked up on Domino's, and it was unwittingly alienating customers with what had become a substandard product. To erode the quality incompetency, Domino's totally revamped its recipes. To enable consumer adoption of the new product, the pizza giant launched a self-deprecating advertising campaign. In the ads, the CEO admitted that the pizza was, in fact, bad, and he committed to fixing it. The campaign worked. Domino's candor worked to ingratiate customers who were then willing to give the new pizza a try. Eroding and enabling factors worked together to get Domino's back on track.

As mentioned earlier, not all enablers are good for business. There is a second type of enabler that works to support or enable incompetencies. These are enemies of value creation and you need to seek them out and eliminate or minimize them. That's essentially what Blockbuster did when it brought Antioco on as CEO. His predecessor, Bill Fields, was an executive at Walmart before accepting the lead position at Blockbuster. Fields brought the wisdom of the world's largest retailer to the Blockbuster chain. There was only one problem: Blockbuster wasn't only in the retail business. Blockbuster was in the entertainment business, but its management largely left that notion behind under Field's leadership. The result was rapid decline in revenue and stock value. When Antioco interviewed for the job, he pointed out the misstep and mapped out a plan to get the company back on track in the entertainment business.

Fields was pursuing the wrong distinctive competencies. That, in turn, created an incompetency, and it took a change of leadership to remove it. As harsh as that may sound, inadvertent incompetencies are not uncommon.

Leaders set organizational direction and company culture and are often the cornerstone of key partnerships. If you have an incompetency in any of these areas, it is quite possible a leader is enabling it. You must be willing to look at these areas with a keen and honest eye and make the hard decisions when necessary. For example, suppose in your start-up you have a partner who just doesn't fit. You're trying to establish a culture of independent thinking and encourage risk and innovation, but your business partner feels the need to micro-manage and is consistently overly critical. Your partner is actually dis-incentivizing the innovation you depend upon and is inadvertently enabling value destruction. As challenging as it may be to address this sort of situation, the consequences of not addressing it are far worse. Enablers of value destruction could eventually undermine your operations, so you need to understand which enablers are the most destructive. You must prioritize and focus your attention.

ENABLERS MATRIX FOR INCOMPETENCIES

DISTINCTIVE INCOMPETENCY ⊖	ERODING FACTOR ⊕ List those with the highest erosion ratings	ENABLING FACTOR List as many enabling factors as you can think of that may support each eroding factor	FREQUENCY OF NEED Scale of 1–10, with 1 being rarely and 10 being daily	IMPACT OF NOT HAVING ENABLER ⊖ Scale of 1–10, with 10 being a profound negative impact on the organization	ENABLING SCORE Frequency multiplied by impact

GENERAL OPERATIONAL ENABLERS
1. List all ways you are enabling incompetencies in your general operations
2. Rate frequency, impact & calculate enabling score

GENERAL ENABLERS OF INCOMPETENCIES ⊖	FREQUENCY OF OCCURRENCE Scale of 1–10, 1 being rarely and 10 being daily	IMPACT OF ENABLER ⊖ Scale of 1–10, with 10 being a profound negative impact	ENABLING SCORE Frequency multiplied by impact

Figure 10: The Enablers Matrix for Incompetencies

Figure 10: The Enablers Matrix for Incompetencies (also found in the resources section and online at ThinkBeyondValue.com) will guide you through the thought process so you can identify and prioritize enablers of incompetencies. Beginning with the top half of the matrix, you will list those eroding factors with the highest erosion ratings from your Erosion Matrix for Incompetencies, being sure to list associated distinctive incompetencies. Then list enabling resources or capabilities you might put in place to help erosion of those incompetencies. Move across each row and rate the frequency of need and impact, then calculate your enabling score. With that done, use the bottom half of the matrix to step back and look for places where you might be directly enabling incompetencies. Be sure to note some key differences when dealing with incompetencies versus competencies in the enablers matrices. Namely, as you rate any general incompetencies, you'll note that you are rating the frequency of occurrence of the enabler and that the impact of general enablers of incompetencies is always negative. You'll rate the frequency of occurrence on a scale of one to ten, with ten being daily. Then you rate how negative the impact is when the enabling of incompetency does occur, with ten being a profoundly negative impact. With these ratings in place, you can calculate your enabling score. Those items with the highest score across the entire matrix (top and bottom) are the enablers that most need your attention.

Remember, as you look about your organization and receive feedback from trusted colleagues and friends, you need to be on the lookout for any damaging enablers of distinctive incompetencies and try to address them. Perhaps you notice that your customer service isn't what it once was. You've developed an incompetency and realize that a leader in that department is enabling poor customer service. Maybe you need to fix that. Or suppose you discover that your production capacity is significantly lower than your peers, and you realize the culprit is a piece of equipment that has never worked properly. That machinery is enabling your distinctive incompetency, and the problem needs to be addressed. New equipment or perhaps a new maintenance plan could erode the incompetency. So, keep considering incompetencies and circling back through the V-REEL Framework as needed to complete the thought processes. And before you are done, bring questions of longevity into the discussion.

How Long before Things Improve?

When you are looking at ways to turn things from destructive to constructive so you can create value in the marketplace, the question of longevity becomes really important. How long are these conditions with my incompetencies going to last? How quickly will the eroding factors help? How long will it take me to activate the eroding factors and the enabling factors that will eliminate or at least minimize these distinctive incompetencies? You can see how the answers to these questions will shape your strategy, right? Suppose you propose a solution to erode an incompetency and then, in considering longevity, realize you'll be sunk before that eroding factor can be put in place. That tells you something. You're going to have to go in another direction. On the other hand, imagine if you can demonstrate that investment in an eroding factor— something like an equipment upgrade—will guarantee a significant boost in production and do so in short order. Your consideration of longevity and presentation of its implications to leadership, or perhaps lenders, may just seal the deal to secure the enabling investment.

Once again, ask the longevity questions regarding our distinctive incompetencies and each of the associated eroding and enabling factors you've considered. For example:

- How long will it take me to raise money?
- How long will it take me to put new equipment in?
- How long will it take me to repay debt?
- How long will it take me to hire a replacement for the person I need to remove?
- Can I last that long?

If the answer to that last question is *no*, maybe you need to look at a different approach to eliminating the distinctive incompetency. Domino's knew it needed to revamp all its recipes and respond to customers' criticism, but it also had to allow enough time to get the recipes right. If it failed to deliver after acknowledging it had a bad product, it might not recover. The company had to keep going while improvements were being made. Domino's could do that. It had the capital to invest in the changes while simultaneously continuing operations. For smaller organizations, that might not always be the case, so you must always ask the longevity questions.

 Consideration of longevity and presentation of its implications to leadership, or perhaps lenders, may just seal the deal to secure needed investment.

Without a doubt, Blockbuster was concerned with longevity when it reached out to Antioco as a potential replacement for Fields. The fact that Antioco had been a studious observer of Blockbuster's decline under Fields meant he had the outline of a turnaround strategy at the interview. He had a keen sense of the problem and was ready to fix it from day one. Antioco didn't have to invest as much time as a less informed candidate, and Blockbuster knew time was of the essence. Antioco hit the ground running with bold changes, and it wasn't long before those changes started paying off.

Like Antioco, Steve Jobs had a keen understanding of what was going wrong at Apple and had a vision for turnaround from the day he returned to the company in 1997. At the time, Apple had a declining 4 percent share of the PC market and had logged annual losses in excess of $1 billion.[52] Jobs forged a strategic partnership with long-time rival

Microsoft, accepted an enabling $150 million capital investment, and ceded the software space to Apple's new partner.[53] With the injection of capital and additional resources freed up from other cancelled programs, Jobs turned his focus to a space he was convinced Microsoft and other players in the PC market would be slow to enter. Jobs set out to define the convergence of communication and computing that would rise with the growth of internet technology. By eliminating areas of incompetency and entering a space that others were not yet considering, Jobs bought Apple both enabling resources and time. The results were staggering. In just fourteen years, Apple went from a $3 billion market capitalization in 1997 to more than $350 billion in 2011.[54]

As you consider longevity related to your distinctive incompetencies, you'll gain clarity on the whole scope of your strategy. Understanding of incompetencies leads to new insights regarding competencies and opportunities for distinctiveness in the marketplace. The various aspects of the V-REEL Framework all work together, weaving a sound strategy strong enough to stand up to harsh competition and flexible enough to respond to a dynamic marketplace.

As we have now completed our overview of the various aspects of the framework and know how to use it to understand both value creation and value destruction, you can pull it all together as a new way of thinking. V-REEL is a framework for strategy formulation, of course, but it is also useful as a common language for teams working toward a common goal and for individuals working to define a path forward. In our final chapter, we will look at practical ways to put V-REEL to work in various situations. My hope is that as we do so you will feel increasingly comfortable and confident with this new vocabulary and that it will prove valuable as you build strategic thinking into the normal operations of your organization. We'll cover more on that in Chapter 7.

Key Steps in Considering Incompetencies

1. SCAN YOUR OPERATIONS WITH AN EYE OUT FOR VALUE
   DESTRUCTION.
   A. WHAT ARE YOUR INCOMPETENCIES?
   B. INVITE TRUSTED COLLEAGUES AND FRIENDS TO SHARE
      INSIGHTS.
2. CONSIDER RARENESS.
   A. ARE YOUR INCOMPETENCIES COMMON AMONG PEERS?
   B. DO YOU HAVE INCOMPETENCIES THAT ARE RARE AMONG
      YOUR PEERS?
   C. TAKE NOTE OF ANY RARE VALUE DESTRUCTION
      (DISTINCTIVE INCOMPETENCIES).
3. COMPLETE THE EROSION MATRIX FOR INCOMPETENCIES.
   A. WHAT ERODING FACTORS CAN YOU PUT INTO PLACE TO
      STOP VALUE DESTRUCTION?
   B. RATE EACH ERODING FACTOR.
   C. CALCULATE EROSION RATINGS AND NOTE THE ERODING
      FACTORS WITH THE HIGHEST RATINGS; THESE ARE YOUR
      MOST IMPORTANT DISTINCTIVE INCOMPETENCIES AND
      ERODING FACTORS.
4. CONSIDER ENABLING FACTORS.
   A. WHAT ENABLERS CAN BE PUT INTO PLACE TO ENCOURAGE
      ERODING FACTORS WITH THE HIGHEST EROSION
      RATINGS?
   B. WHAT GENERAL ENABLERS OF INCOMPETENCIES NEED
      TO BE ELIMINATED?
   C. USE THE ENABLERS MATRIX FOR INCOMPETENCIES TO
      INVENTORY AND PRIORITIZE.

5. STEP BACK AND LOOK AT ALL INCOMPETENCIES, AND ASK THE LONGEVITY QUESTIONS.

   A. HOW LONG BEFORE THINGS CHANGE?

   B. WHAT PRIORITIES NEED TO BE ADJUSTED GIVEN YOUR ANSWERS?

   C. DO YOU HAVE ENOUGH TIME?

   D. GIVEN YOUR ANSWERS, PRIORITIZE.

CHAPTER 7

Onward and Upward! V-REEL for the Win

I f you've ever gone through the process of writing a proposal—any kind of proposal—you know how great it feels to turn it in. You feel like you've accomplished something. Then one day—if you're lucky—you find out you got it! You won the bid, got the grant, secured the contract. The thrill is palpable! At least for a few seconds. Then, elation turns to dread, maybe even panic. Now you must do the work. But no need to panic about the work of V-REEL. This chapter is here to help you get started and avoid the dread. You've done the work of getting familiar with V-REEL. You've read this far, so using the V-REEL Framework in your situation will come more naturally than you might think. The V-REEL Framework provides a new way of thinking about strategy and even about life. My charge to you is to accept what I call the V-REEL Challenge. I am inviting you to be more thorough in your strategy formulation than perhaps you have been in the past. The framework prompts you to think beyond value and seek rareness in the marketplace. It challenges you to work through eroding factors and enable your organization to succeed. V-REEL even prompts you to consider how you might be destroying value. And finally, this framework encourages you to consider how dynamic the marketplace really is and ask yourself if you have enough time to create real value. Perhaps most difficult of all, V-REEL will nudge you to walk away from the ideas that just don't work. All of that is the V-REEL Challenge. And like most challenges, this one has its own rewards.

After all, don't we all want to create value? We all hope to somehow make the world better and use our unique talents and resources to earn a living, certainly, but even more importantly, to be of value. I believe that's true of most people, and that's part of the reason I wrote this book. Most people want to be at their best, do their best, and find success. Creating value is essential to achieving those goals, no matter what your day-to-day life looks like. By now, I hope you can see how V-REEL will help you be your best, create personal value and, of course, create value in your professional life as well. In this closing chapter of *Think Beyond Value*, I will provide additional insight into how you can apply V-REEL in your professional situation and even in your personal life.

 Most people want to be their best, do their best, and find success. Creating value is essential to achieving those goals.

Many of the people I've worked with have shared how, more than anything else, V-REEL changed the way they think about their businesses and even their personal strategies. A good friend and very successful consultant realized that she was her own eroding factor. She had structured her business around her competencies, which was great until she faced the reality that she is, in fact, only one person and, therefore, limited in how she can create value for customers. Another company benefitted from the framework's simple terminology, using it to improve communication across teams. That's really great to hear, and I'm grateful that the work of creating V-REEL and sharing it with others is proving useful. I'm convinced that one of the reasons the framework works is because it is simple, and the language of V-REEL is easy to remember and understand. But I also know that understanding V-REEL and putting the framework into action are as different as writing the proposal and executing the project. So, I want to invite you to engage in the V-REEL Challenge. I am challenging you to pick up this mantle—this way of thinking about your personal and professional value creation—and run with it. Make it work for you and for your teams as you work through the framework all the way to the win. V-REEL can get you to the win because, when fully implemented, the framework leaves little room for mediocrity. You are going for distinctiveness—value *and* rareness, protected against erosion and enabled for longevity. That is special. That is how you win. To help you get started, here are some practical ways you can put V-REEL to work for you.

What You Know Now—V-REEL in Review

I've covered a good bit of information in the last several chapters, so let's review. Figure 11: The V-REEL Framework for Strategy Formulation shows the entire V-REEL Framework, so you can refer to that as we review. Value is good, but it's not quite good enough to get you to a win in the marketplace. You also need some degree of rareness to create real value that wins. When you find resources and capabilities that are both valuable and have some degree of rareness in the marketplace, you have potential distinctive competencies. And that's when things start to get interesting. Until then—until you can look at your external and internal environments and say with some degree of confidence that your offering is both valuable *and* rare—you need to stay within the value and rareness loop. Do not pass go. Do not collect your money. Stay put. Work the *V* and the *R*. Find those distinctive competencies. It's worth the effort, because you know both value and rareness are required to create any real value in the marketplace. Starting to feel the challenge?

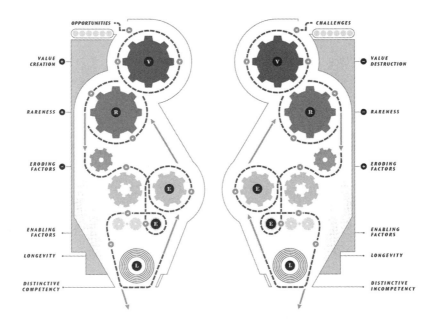

Figure 11: The V-REEL Framework for Strategy Formulation

Once you've identified potential distinctive competencies, you're ready to move on to consider eroding factors, enabling factors, and longevity. Notice that I put all of those together in one sentence. You may recall the natural inclination to almost immediately begin thinking about enabling factors when you identify an eroding factor. It's intuitive. You know you need to think about this. You want to protect against erosion of value creation and so your mind naturally goes to enabling factors to defend against erosion. But take the time to prioritize first. Use your Erosion Matrix for Competencies to inventory potential distinctive competencies and list potential eroding factors. Calculate your erosion ratings then move to the Enablers Matrix for Competencies to list potential enabling factors for the eroding factors with the highest erosion ratings. If you cannot put enablers in place to defend against eroding factors with the highest erosion ratings, step back. Ask yourself the hard questions: Do you need to walk away? Can you define different distinctive competencies? If you can build up enablers to defend against erosion, then ask yourself how long it will take to do so. Do you have enough time?

Longevity is the goal. You want to create real value long enough to justify the investment. If you can, great! Keep going through the framework (you know there's more). But if you don't find that you have viable distinctive competencies given the eroding and enabling factors *and* longevity, stop. Stop confidently, proudly even, and return to value and rareness and find new potential distinctive competencies and put those to the test. Keep working V-REEL. You know how to think through real value-creating opportunities—considering rareness, eroding and enabling factors—to develop strategies with enough longevity to create real value in the marketplace. So keep working V-REEL. This is the way to win.

You've done the good work of identifying enabling resources and capabilities to defend against erosion. You've determined that you can put those enabling resources into place quickly enough to allow the longevity you need to create value. Now you need to enable your business operations. Consider your operational strategy. Given your resources and capabilities, all the eroding factors, the enablers, and the amount of time you have, determine what general business strategy makes sense for you. Do you need more information? Additional expertise? If so, go get it. It is all part of the V-REEL Challenge.

 Value is good, but it's not quite good enough to get you to a win in the marketplace. You also need some degree of rareness to create real value that wins.

Having considered value and rareness and worked through erosion and enabling factors, and having determined how to enable your operational strategy, it is time to step back and consider longevity. To some extent, you've thought about this already in terms of individual eroding and enabling factors, but now you need to step back and look at the big picture. How much time do you have? Given everything you've considered, is it enough time to achieve a competitive advantage—to create superior value in the market? If so, great! If not, can you do anything about it? If you have the potential for a competitive advantage, is there a way to widen the window of time for that potential? These are hard questions, particularly at this stage, because you've invested a lot of thinking and research in your idea. Even so, if you do not know with some degree of confidence that you have enough time to create value, then the best course of action may be to return to the drawing board. Maybe you need to find a better idea that provides enough time to win.

In some sense, I think this may be the most challenging point in the framework because you have invested considerably to get to this point, and you've likely shared your idea with a lot of people. Walking away from your idea takes courage, but at this point you probably know if that's what you need to do. The temptation is strong to move forward anyway and just figure things out as you go. I believe wholeheartedly that is the very sort of decision that leads to a significant number of business failures. It is far wiser to take the challenging path of walking away and shaping a stronger opportunity than to go down a path that you know in your gut is too short to get you to a win.

 It is far wiser to take the challenging path of walking away and shaping a stronger opportunity than to go down a path that you know in your gut is too short to get you to a win.

But not everyone will be faced with that decision. Many, having worked through iterations of value and rareness along with erosion and enabling factors, will step back from all they've learned, consider longevity, and determine that time is on their side. When that's the case, it is time to move on to the final step of the V-REEL Challenge and consider incompetencies. This pass through the V-REEL Framework is critical. It is where you identify and address those areas where value destruction could wreak havoc. You do so to avoid having so much destruction going on that you can't create value. It's important and worthwhile. That's why you work through value and rareness again, this time looking for value destruction that's rare in your marketplace. Recall that rareness is a bad thing when we are talking about incompetencies because you don't want to be the only one in the contest with a devastating incompetency. You seek out those rare incompetencies and make note of them in your Erosion Matrix for Incompetencies. You then note ways that you might erode each rare incompetency.

Having done that, you once again calculate the potential impact of each eroding factor. This allows you to prioritize and use the Enablers

Matrix for Incompetencies to focus on enabling those eroding factors with the greatest potential for eliminating or minimizing distinctive incompetencies. Finally, you consider how long it will take to address incompetencies and what impact your answers will have on the longevity of your value creation. All this new information supports your entire strategy, providing you with a clear picture of what you need to focus on first.

In the end, having worked through the V-REEL Framework considering first your competencies and then your incompetencies, you will find you have a clear sense of those which are distinctive. You will understand what you need to do to protect and enable distinctive competencies and how long you have to do it. And you will understand your distinctive *in*comptencies and what you need to do to minimize or eliminate them. In short, you will have a plan. Equally as important, you will have a great deal of insight to support that plan. You can move forward with confidence. This is the aim of the V-REEL Challenge, and as you have seen, it is indeed a challenge. You are pushing yourself to work through the entire V-REEL Framework, first doing the big work of considering value creation and then working through the framework a second time to address any value destruction. By accepting the V-REEL Challenge and working all the way through the framework, you are giving yourself the benefit of great insights and the best possible chance for a win.

Knowing all this, maybe you're wondering how to get others using V-REEL so you can work together to shape sound strategy. Perhaps you want to get your entire team working with a common set of terms that facilitate communication, productive dialogue, and sound decision making. Or maybe you're wondering how V-REEL might work to help you think through personal goals. In the section that follows, I'll offer suggested approaches to putting V-REEL to work in a variety of scenarios so you are ready to bring your team to the conversation or just think through your own personal strategy. Let's get started putting V-REEL to work for the win.

Putting V-REEL to Work for You

The V-REEL Framework has value for entrepreneurs, of course, and is also quite useful in corporate environments and among business units. It can be applied to existing or new for-profits and not-for-profits alike, and can be very useful for individuals. There are some subtle differences in how you might approach V-REEL in each situation, so I'll discuss those briefly here.

V-REEL for Established Businesses

Existing businesses and corporations may have a bit of an advantage going into the V-REEL Framework as compared to a start-up or an entrepreneur looking to flesh out and evaluate a new business idea. As an existing business, you already have at least some sense of what your customers value and are willing to purchase. Existing businesses know that customers like this or value that. You likely even know what your customers *don't* like, and that is very good to know, especially when it comes time to consider value destruction. As someone operating within an existing business environment looking to put V-REEL to work, how might you start? I like to start by asking a question: How do you create value? It is important to really think about your answers and to be very explicit about how you create value for customers. And since you really do need to think this through, it is a good idea to bring in your team members to get them in on the conversation. You might consider providing them with a brief introduction to V-REEL—maybe walk them through the framework—and then dive in and start asking questions.

How do you create value? What is it that keeps your customers coming back? Start with what first comes to mind and then dig a bit deeper. Maybe spend some time thinking about other ways you might be able to create value for customers. Consider some of the things we discussed in the book that you hadn't thought about before. Are there intangibles at work creating value that perhaps you previously overlooked? Start with what you know or are readily aware of, and then think how you might add to that list of ways you create value.

From there, an existing business can use the framework to help verify current strategy, its viability, and longevity. And having considered longevity, the business can then think about what it needs to do, given that the current strategy is only going to produce value for a determined period. Applying the V-REEL Framework, an existing business might realize that it needs to take quick action to stop the damaging effects of an eroding factor and extend the life of a distinctive competency. Similarly, leaders might realize the need to invest six months to clean up an incompetency identified in the second pass through the framework. Ideally, by working through the framework, an existing business will recognize how it is creating value *right now*. It will discover ways to extend the life of that value creation and begin to see new opportunities to explore and exploit. This will allow the business to continue to create value when the current strategy is no longer viable.

 Using the V-REEL Framework, existing businesses will recognize how they are creating value now and discover new opportunities to explore and exploit.

To achieve that level of insight through the framework, it is best if your entire team adopts the language of V-REEL and applies the framework to everyday strategic thinking. Imagine tasking your team to brainstorm ideas for new products or services. Applying the language of V-REEL and working through the framework, that team can come back to you having thought critically through ideas until they have something that really has a chance to win in the marketplace. And that is the goal. Back in the introduction of this book, I talked about the corporate cry for critical thinking skills. V-REEL can help your team think critically. Whether you're a middle manager working to execute divisional operations or an executive looking to transform corporate thinking, I hope you'll use V-REEL to help form critical thinkers and shape winning strategy.

V-REEL for Entrepreneurs

Start-up companies, like their corporate counterparts, are looking to shape winning strategy. But the entrepreneur generally doesn't have the advantage of existing customers—at least not at the beginning. If you have existing customers, you have some sense of what they value. But entrepreneurs are typically trying to find customers, so they are in this constant effort to discover what prospective customers value and then deliver it. The V-REEL Challenge to entrepreneurs is this: think beyond the value proposition *before* you go all in on your big idea. For a lot of entrepreneurs, that requires a great deal of restraint. Big ideas are exciting! They often come with a sense of urgency, and many entrepreneurs mistake that sense of urgency as the opportunity for a head start on the best new deal in town. With V-REEL, I am challenging entrepreneurs to hold on just a bit and really consider the idea. Is it rare? Will eroding factors come along to take away that rareness? If so, can you put enablers into place soon enough to stop eroding factors, protect your distinctive competencies, and achieve a competitive advantage?

By now you know all the questions entrepreneurs need to ask, but starting this process for entrepreneurs will naturally be a bit challenging. Why? Because there is a good bit of work involved in understanding the market, getting familiar with customer behaviors, and identifying competitors. Existing businesses know this from experience. Entrepreneurs must go out and find the information. Working through the framework may take a bit more time for entrepreneurs, but cycling through value and rareness until you come up with something that has potential for distinctiveness is worthwhile. It sets you up on a path that could lead to success. Continuing through the framework to identify eroding and enabling factors, and considering the longevity of your big idea serves to further refine it, honing it into something that might work.

 It may take a bit of time to work through the V-REEL Framework, but cycling through value and rareness until you come up with something that has potential for distinctiveness is worthwhile.

For entrepreneurs, V-REEL is perhaps most valuable as a strategy formulation tool. If used from the beginning and fully exercised, the framework can shed light on weaknesses in your big idea and help identify ways to bolster it. V-REEL can also be useful if you think you've already formed a strong strategy, but you want to make sure you're ready for a big pitch to prospective investors. You know they will have hard questions, and V-REEL is a great tool to use to help you anticipate and answer those questions as you prepare your pitch. But perhaps the most valuable aspect of V-REEL is its potential to keep you from proceeding with a big idea that just doesn't have the makings of a winning business. V-REEL can help expose the holes in a strategy, and it will help you see if those holes are too big to fill. Remember the spoiler alert from early in the book? You should walk away from most ideas. Entrepreneurs don't like to hear that; they like walking away even less. But those that do walk away from the ideas that just can't work usually find themselves on a new path full of potential opportunity. Use V-REEL to get you on the path to win.

V-REEL for Not-for-Profit Organizations

Whether starting up or already ongoing, not-for-profits have much in common with their for-profit counterparts. If you're working within an existing not-for-profit, you likely have a good sense of what your various stakeholders value, so you have some advantage going into the V-REEL Challenge. Or if you're starting up a new not-for-profit organization, you probably have some work ahead of you to really understand how best to lend value to whatever issue you are seeking to address. But when formulating strategy, there are two considerations that not-for-profits will face that differ from those of for-profits. First, as a not-for-profit, you have something of a bi-directional value proposition. That is, you must create value both for those you seek to serve and for those who provide the resources that enable you to provide that service. And second, when considering longevity, it is possible that you will need to approach this entirely differently than for-profits, especially if your aim is to eliminate the problem your organization was established to address. Let's look at value creation in the not-for-profit setting first.

 Not-for-profit organizations must create value both for those they seek to serve and for those who provide the resources that enable them to provide that service.

As a not-for-profit organization, you are beholden to at least two sets of customers: those you serve because of your mission and those whose resources you rely upon to pursue that mission. As a result, you really need to consider your value proposition, rareness, enablers, eroding factors, and longevity for both sets of customers. You have a bit more work to do than your for-profit counterparts, but V-REEL can help you get to a clear path forward. The framework can shape your thinking so that you remain aware of and responsive to your situation with both those you serve and those who enable you to serve. As you employ V-REEL, you will need to work through the framework twice. Initially, to determine if you have distinctive competencies regarding the work directly related to your mission and, subsequently, to consider what sort of value you might create for your funding entities so they continue to see the value in funding your mission.

Not-for-profits have a tough job because, on the one hand, they are trying to achieve a mission, and on the other hand, trying to show the value of that mission to those with the ability to fund them. These could be two very different audiences and as such need to be considered separately. You're still creating value, but the way that you're portraying and communicating that is going to be different depending on the stakeholder to whom you are talking. When you're thinking about going into this process from a not-for-profit standpoint, you've got a different type of homework to do than an existing for-profit business; for example, you need to think about what you want to accomplish with your mission, of course, but also how you will communicate the value of that to supporters, donors, and contributors in a manner that will keep them engaged and, very importantly, supporting your organization. And it is quite possible that those stakeholders will want to have some influence over how the organization creates value with the group or issue you are aiming to serve. You can see how this can get complicated rather quickly. Existing not-for-profits know this all too well and can use the V-REEL Framework to better articulate and refine what they are doing to create value for each set of customers. Working through the framework will expose where you might need to change things and provide a sense of what you might be able to do in the future.

Longevity is, of course, all about the future. How far will the distinctiveness you enjoy today take you into the future? Can you extend that timeframe? In the case of the not-for-profit, how long do you need to achieve your mission? It is conceivable that some not-for-profits would be so effective in pursuit of their missions that they would work themselves out of a job. In these cases, considerations of longevity need to be made with that in mind. If your mission is such that you can solve the problem you set out to address, then your considerations of longevity would focus on sustaining operations long enough to achieve that goal. You still ask all the questions about longevity when you're considering eroding and enabling factors because you need to know how those factors might affect the life of your value proposition. You also step back once you have addressed those individual questions, look at the whole picture, and ask how long you need to achieve the mission. If you only need to function for a limited period, that will have a significant impact on all aspects of your operation including your message to supporters. If, on the other hand, your mission requires ongoing operations to meet your objective and provide value to those you serve, then your considerations of longevity will look more like the typical for-profit organization. Whatever the case for your situation, V-REEL will help you shape a strategy for delivering value to all the stakeholders over whatever timeframe is needed to achieve your mission.

V-REEL for Individuals

Each of us, as individuals, has something of value to offer the world. Maybe you bring some aspect of that value to the workplace, or perhaps your value is found most at home, at church, or in the community. Wherever you are, you have the potential to add value. And that's why V-REEL makes sense as a tool for individuals seeking to improve their positions at work, considering a new career, or even just trying to feel a sense of personal value. A young person trying to decide a course of study or a career path could use V-REEL to explore the possibilities and define a path forward. Remember the history major who didn't consider the employment market? V-REEL might have helped him see the need for a teaching certificate or graduate school. Similarly, someone looking for a change in career will find V-REEL a useful framework for considering the next move. Even a retiree who isn't quite sure how to give back to the community can find clarity through the V-REEL Framework.

When working with an individual to map out a personal plan or strategy, one of the first things I want to do is find out if the person has ever considered what he or she is doing right now. Have you ever thought about how you create value? When faced with this question, most people immediately think about their skills and abilities. They might name previous jobs. Young people tend to talk about their best subjects in school. That's a good start, but there is more to personal value creation than a set of skills, a résumé, or an academic transcript. Think about how you are creating value for other people right now. What is it that you are doing that's potentially rare? What eroding factors are going to come along and affect that? What are the enablers you can put into place, so that you can continue to create that value?

Individuals hoping to use V-REEL to define plans for the future should run through the framework considering their current situations. Until you understand where you are now, it is very difficult to think about making any sort of changes. V-REEL can help identify what you have to work with and what you might need to acquire. And just as entrepreneurs sometimes need to walk away from a big idea, individuals may find they simply do not have the resources—or cannot acquire them in time—to pursue a chosen path. And that's good to know before you go too far down the wrong path.

Individuals hoping to use V-REEL to define plans for the future should run through the framework considering their current situations. V-REEL can help identify what you have to work with and what you might need to acquire.

Imagine that a high school student spends some time working through the V-REEL Framework to consider career options. The value and rareness discussion begins with understanding what each student values, his or her academic and work skills, and even an understanding of personality traits. If a student values working with a team or being outdoors or has a big personality, he or she might consider careers that require those things. The student will then need to consider what qualities are rare or that in some way set the student apart from the crowd. Perhaps the student is bi-lingual or really enjoys volunteering with the elderly. With these things in mind, a student can explore the external environment and get a sense of what careers are available, the educational requirements, and so on, and then determine what might need to be done to become the most valuable person to prospective employers. The student might realize that poor grades in high school will erode opportunities to attend the best school for his or her favorite major. Another student may discover that he or she needs to take some additional science classes to qualify for their university of choice. Asking the longevity question will help high school students understand if they have enough time to prepare for the university or career in which they're interested before they graduate, or if they need an alternative plan.

This example for a high school student is simple, perhaps, but it is also empowering. V-REEL can help people of all ages think critically about their current situations and any ideas they might have for change. The framework prompts people to question their assumptions, and in doing so, they gain insights that inform good decisions. Maybe you recognize that you have certain resources and capabilities you're not fully exploiting. If you're looking to make a change, you might consider how you could exploit those resources and capabilities to create value. Or you might realize that you don't have much with which to work in the way of capabilities relevant to that job you've dreamed about for years. Knowing that, you can decide to invest in developing new skills and enable that investment by allowing yourself the time you need. Taking the V-REEL Challenge will help you see possibilities—possibilities you might not have known existed. Many people might be doing some of this intuitively, but the V-REEL Framework challenges you to be more proactive. It is a challenge to think intentionally about how you make decisions, how you approach a career, and how you consider your future.

A Clear Path Forward

The V-REEL Framework is a platform for thinking about change—in an existing organization, a new business, or in your personal life. Change is inevitable and very often unwelcome, but most of the time it doesn't have to be a surprise. To think beyond value is to think about how you create value today and accept the challenge to consider value creation in the context of our ever-changing world. The intent is that you will anticipate what's coming and either prepare to take advantage of it or get out of harm's way. But make no mistake: a willingness to step off a path is not the same as a fear of failure. Using the V-REEL Framework does not eliminate risk; it prepares you for it. The V-REEL Challenge encourages innovation by prompting you to acknowledge shortfalls and return to the beginning, if necessary, to seek a better plan forward.

In the next sections of the book you will find resources to help you as you put V-REEL to work for you. I've created a glossary so you can get a quick refresher of the ideas that we've discussed. You'll also find a quick start guide to V-REEL. This summary of the concepts to consider will guide you to create your strategy and articulate next steps. In Resources, I've included blank versions of the erosion and enabling matrices for competencies and incompetencies so you can copy and complete them with your teams. The same forms are available to download online at ThinkBeyondValue.com. Finally, for those who wish to go even deeper into V-REEL or stay fresh on this approach to strategic thinking, I invite you to follow our team online, participate in workshops, and join us at speaking engagements.

By adopting the V-REEL Framework, you're providing yourself and your team with both a structure to guide planning and a language to facilitate communication. You're investing in the process of strategy formulation and enabling sound reasoning. The rewards are clarity, decisiveness, and, with a little luck, a win. Will you accept the challenge?

CHALLENGE ACCEPTED!

If you're determined to accept the V-REEL Challenge (and I hope you are), I want you to know you'll have support along the way. Strategy formulation is a journey and, as with most journeys, this one is far more enjoyable and fruitful with friends. There is much we can learn from one another as we build a community of strategic thinkers. In this modern age, there are many ways to stay connected and share ideas, so I invite you to visit my website ThinkBeyondValue.com. But more importantly, I encourage you to engage with me online. On Twitter, I will be commenting from time to time on headlines and, where possible, I will respond to the comments and questions of any followers in the twitter-verse. Likewise, on Facebook, I'll share blogs with new insights and keep friends informed of upcoming speaking engagements, workshops, and new online resources. But know this: the true potential of thinking beyond value rests in you, the readers, thinkers, entrepreneurs, leaders, and world changers. As you think beyond value and adopt the V-REEL mindset, you will not only improve your own opportunities, but you will very likely begin to speak differently. Others may notice and be curious. I hope you'll use the simple yet powerful language of V-REEL to help others find clarity. The fact is, I don't know the full potential of this framework, but I'd like to explore the power of V-REEL through your implementation of the framework and your sharing of successes and struggles. So, let's begin a conversation and build a community. Let's go for the win together. Ask questions, share successes, and let me know about any struggles. I will do my best to offer guidance through online communities and, perhaps, have the pleasure of meeting you in person.

Until then, Shalom.

Find and follow David online at:

DrDavidFlint.com
Twitter: DrDavidFlint
Facebook: DrDavidFlint
LinkedIn: DavidFlint

ABOUT THE AUTHOR

David Flint is a professor, mentor, musician, world traveler, dog walker, and, as an entrepreneur, a habitual risk taker. He also enjoys regularly attending Texas A&M football games each fall. David has been engaged in entrepreneurial activities since the early 1980s across multiple industries and is presently involved in board or leadership positions across business endeavors in software applications, real estate, and insurance. David serves on the boards of several not-for-profit organizations with both domestic and international activities and is passionate about helping businesses, entrepreneurs, and individuals succeed.

Though he originally developed his V-REEL Framework to aid his teaching of strategy formulation, David has since used the tool in support of consulting engagements, helping companies of all sizes think beyond the value proposition and form clear go-forward strategies. As a public speaker, facilitator, and consultant, David is now working to bring the framework to bear on the efforts of for- and not-for-profit enterprises in the United States and internationally.

David brings a rich diversity of education and experience to every conversation and engagement. His eclectic educational background includes study of history, computer science, and international management and culminated with a PhD from Texas A&M University in management focused on business-government relationships. Today, David enjoys speaking and consulting when he is not teaching strategic management and entrepreneurship at Texas A&M University.

GLOSSARY OF TERMS

competency bundle: much like a cable, which is really made up of a bundle of smaller cables, a competency bundle is a group of competencies, resources, and capabilities bound together such that they form something potentially distinctive in the marketplace

competencies: composed of tangible and/or intangible resources and the capabilities to use those resources; things that have the potential to create value for you or your organization

competitive advantage: a superior value-creating position in the marketplace which can be measured using comparable returns

competitive disadvantage: an inferior value-creating position in the marketplace which can be measured using comparable returns

competitive parity: a neutral value-creating position in the marketplace which results in the same performance as competitors and can be measured using comparable returns

core competencies: things you or your organization do particularly well and are the focus for and key drivers of creating value; not to be confused with distinctive competencies

distinctive competencies: core competencies—and/or a competency bundle—that allow an individual or organization to create value in the marketplace *and* that are rare and unlikely to be imitated or substituted by competitors

distinctive incompetencies: incompetencies that destroy an individual's or organization's ability to create value in the marketplace *and* that are rare and unlikely to be imitated or substituted by competitors

economies of scale: savings in costs achieved by increased levels of production such that the average cost of producing your product or service decreases

economies of scope: savings gained by producing two or more distinct products and/or services when the cost of doing so is less than producing them separately

enabling factors for competencies: resources and capabilities that protect against eroding factors for competencies and/or make it possible for your organization to operate

enabling factors for incompetencies: 1. resources and capabilities that support eroding factors for incompetencies, 2. resources and capabilities that inadvertently serve to increase incompetencies

eroding factors for competencies: anything that diminishes your organization's ability to create value or remain rare in the marketplace

eroding factors for incompetencies: anything that diminishes your organization's incompetencies

five forces analysis: Porter's model provides a mechanism for understanding and analyzing the level of competition within an industry to aid business strategy development. Of concern, according to Porter's Five Forces, are threat of substitute products or services, threat of established rivals, threat of new entrants, the bargaining power of suppliers, and the bargaining power of customers

incompetencies: composed of tangible and/or intangible resources and the capabilities to use those resources; things inside you or your organization that have the potential to destroy value and/or rareness

market factors: conditions that are directly and immediately related to your specific business activities in your industry; examples include the available workforce; demographic characteristics of customers in the target market; the cost of supplies, office space, and equipment; availability of capital; competing products or services from existing competitors

network externality effect: the effect of a user of a product or service on the value of that product or service; for example, this effect is at play with social networks like Facebook where value increases as the number of users increases

non-market factors: general, more distant conditions that could impact your organization in indirect ways; examples include politics, the economy, sociocultural trends, or changes in technology

primary activities: in Porter's value chain analysis, primary activities are those activities undertaken in an organization that are directly related to value creation

rareness: a resource and/or capability has rareness when it is uncommon or unique in the marketplace; rareness is essential to value creation

resource-based view of the firm: a model for understanding your resources and capabilities and how they might come together to form distinctive competencies

social capital: the networks of relationships among people who live and work in a specific community; social capital is often comprised of an organization's supporters and champions in the community

strategic management: strategic management is the formulation and implementation of the major goals and initiatives undertaken by a company's top management on behalf of owners given consideration of resources, and an assessment of the organization's internal and external environments

strategy formulation: the process by which an organization chooses the most appropriate courses of action to achieve its defined goals

supporting activities: in Porter's value chain analysis, supporting activities are those activities undertaken in an organization that are not directly related to value creation but are necessary for operation

switching costs: costs associated with changing to a new product or service; examples include retraining, new hardware, and new facilities that must be built

V-REEL Framework: a mnemonic device and process for thinking through a value proposition, its organizational and strategic context, and to help determine what (if any) potential exists to achieve a sustainable competitive advantage in the marketplace; the V-REEL letters stand for value, rareness, eroding factors, enabling factors, and longevity

VRIS framework: a series of questions in the resource-based view of the firm that you can ask about a resource, capability, or competency to understand how potentially important it might be in regard to an ability to create value. Is it valuable? Is it rare? Is it difficult to imitate? Is it difficult to substitute?

value: the perception on the part of customers that a product, service, or experience is worth more than the money it costs to create

value chain analysis: Michael Porter's approach to looking at the internal activities employed by an organization in the process of creating and delivering value

value proposition: a statement of how an organization intends to create value in the marketplace

V-REEL QUICK START GUIDE

Use this guide to help you and your team work through the entire V-REEL Framework. When you've made it through, you will have completed the nine critical steps to strategy formulation.

1. Identify distinctive competencies.
2. Prioritize eroding factors for distinctive competencies.
3. Prioritize enabling factors for distinctive competencies.
4. Consider the longevity of distinctive competencies.
5. Identify distinctive incompetencies.
6. Prioritize eroding factors for distinctive incompetencies.
7. Prioritize enabling factors for distinctive incompetencies.
8. Consider the longevity of distinctive incompetencies.
9. Assess your potential for competitive advantage.

Once you complete the nine steps, you should have a good idea if and how to move forward. Use the V-REEL Framework for Strategy Formulation to help you think through value and rareness, eroding factors, enabling factors, and longevity. The framework will guide you as you complete all nine steps and find a sense of confidence and clarity that comes from sound strategic thinking.

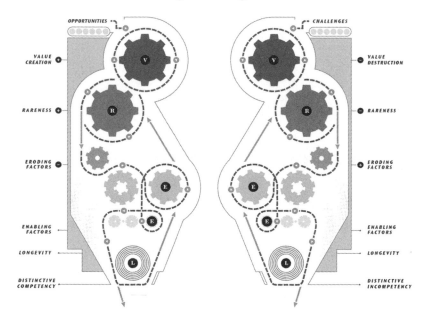

The V-REEL Framework for Strategy Formulation

Value and Rareness

Complete the following steps and keep working through considerations of value creation and rareness until you have a strong sense of the resources and capabilities that might set you apart from the competition. Resources and capabilities that are both valuable and rare and contribute to your ability to create value in the marketplace are potential distinctive competencies. Be sure to take note of any you uncover. You'll know you're ready to move past value and rareness to consider eroding factors when you've identified a least a few *potential* distinctive competencies.

1. Articulate your value proposition.

2. Inventory the resources and capabilities you need to create value.

3. Consider your external environment.

   a. Market factors

   b. Non-market factors

   c. Bargaining power of suppliers

   d. Bargaining power of buyers

   e. Threat of substitutes

   f. Threat of new entrants

   g. Rivalry

4. Consider your internal environment and use the following tools as appropriate:

   a. Resource-Based View

   b. VRIS framework

   c. Competency Bundle

5. Document potential distinctive competencies (valuable + rare) in the left column of the Erosion Matrix for Competencies.

Eroding Factors

You begin consideration of eroding factors with potential distinctive competencies. As you reconsider each of these potential sources of value creation in respect to erosion, you may begin to sense that what you thought was distinctive isn't able to stand up to the forces of erosion in the external environment or even within your organization. That's okay. Work through the following steps. Even if it begins to feel like your big idea is losing ground, go ahead and calculate erosion ratings and prioritize your eroding factors. Then move on to consider if enabling factors can stabilize things.

1. Begin with your potential distinctive competencies (valuable + rare).

2. Consider potential eroding factors for each distinctive competency.

    a. Consider imitation, substitution, obsolescence, depletion, etc.

    b. Consider non-market factors as sources of erosion (political, regulatory, etc.).

    c. Consider market factors as sources of erosion (rivalry, etc.).

3. Complete the Erosion Matrix for Competencies.

    a. List potential distinctive competencies.

    b. List potential eroding factors for each distinctive competency.

    c. Rate the likely occurrence of each factor.

    d. Rate the potential impact of each factor.

    e. Calculate your erosion ratings.

4. Note eroding factors with the highest erosion ratings.

Enabling Factors

As you were completing the Erosion Matrix for Competencies, you may have naturally begun thinking about enabling factors to defend against erosion. If so, you have a good start on your Enablers Matrix for Competencies. Work through the following steps and remember that following the path back to value and rareness as needed is a step in the right direction if viable enablers are not coming to mind. You'll know you're ready to move on to considerations of longevity when you have identified viable enablers to defend against your eroding factors with the highest erosion ratings.

1. Begin with your Erosion Matrix, focusing on items with the highest erosion ratings.

2. List enabling factors to defend against each of the erosion factors with the highest ratings.
    a. If you can identify workable enablers against erosion, move on to step three below.
    b. If you are not able to identify viable enablers to defend against eroding factors, return to value and rareness to identify potential distinctive competencies.
3. Identify operational enablers.
    a. Consider your general business strategy (cost leadership or differentiation).
    b. Seek out additional information as needed to educate yourself on topics such as business-level strategy, corporate-level strategy, accounting, finance, and human resource management.
    c. List additional enablers needed to support your operation.
4. Prioritize—Use the enablers matrix for competencies.
    a. List enablers in the Enablers Matrix for Competencies.
    b. Rate the frequency and impact of each enabler and calculate the enabler rating.
    c. Enablers with the highest enabler rating should receive highest priority.

Longevity

If you've made it this far, your distinctive competencies might just be taking shape, but you need to consider that the world is a dynamic place, and things will change. Take the time to work through the following steps and don't hesitate to go back and reconsider eroding factors, enablers, and even rareness and value if need be to shape a strong strategy. You'll know you're ready to move on to consider distinctive incompetencies when you can step back and look at potential distinctive competencies and feel confident that you have or can put in place necessary enabling factors.

1. Review what you know:
   a. Scan the external environment.
   b. Scan the internal environment.
2. Ask the longevity questions.
   a. How long before the external environment changes?
   b. How long before things change in the internal environment?
3. Revisit eroding and enabling factors and ask:
   a. How long before erosion sets in?
      i. Can you do anything about it?
      ii. If so, how does that affect your longevity?
   b. How long before you can put enabling resources into place?
      i. Can you get them in place soon enough?
      ii. If so, how does that affect longevity?
4. Consider the whole picture and ask:
   a. What priorities need to be adjusted given your responses to the longevity questions?
   b. Do you have enough time?
5. Given your answers to the longevity questions, prioritize.
   a. What do you need to do first?
   b. What do you need to do second?
   c. And so on…

Consider Incompetencies

With a solid set of distinctive competencies well defended against erosion, it's time to flip and repeat. Turn your attention to the other side of the V-REEL Framework and consider how you might be destroying your ability to create value in the marketplace. Follow these steps to work through the V-REEL Framework to overcome those distinctive incompetencies that most threaten your value and rareness in the marketplace.

1. Scan your operations with an eye out for value destruction.
   a. What are your incompetencies?
   b. Invite trusted colleagues and friends to share insights.
2. Consider rareness.
   a. Are your incompetencies common among peers?
   b. Do you have incompetencies that are rare among your peers?
   c. Take note of any rare value destruction (distinctive incompetencies).
3. Complete the Erosion Matrix for Incompetencies.
   a. What eroding factors can you put in place to stop value destruction?
   b. Rate each eroding factor.
      i. How likely is it that you can put the eroding factor into place?
      ii. Assuming the eroding factor is implemented, how significantly will it impact your organization?
   c. Calculate erosion ratings and note the eroding factors with the highest ratings; these are your most important distinctive incompetencies and eroding factors.
4. Consider enabling factors using the Enablers Matrix for Incompetencies.
   a. What enablers can be put into place to encourage eroding factors with the highest erosion ratings?
   b. What general enablers need to be eliminated to minimize incompetencies?

5. Step back and look at all incompetencies and ask the longevity questions.

    a. How long before things change?

    b. What priorities need to be adjusted given your answers?

    c. Do you have enough time?

    d. Given your answers, prioritize.

Assess Your Competitive Advantage…If You Have One

You've done a lot of work thinking about your big idea, refining it to build greater value and rareness and imagining how you can build up enabling factors to defend against erosion and run an effective operation. Finally, you are ready to step back and look at the whole picture—distinctive competencies and distinctive incompetencies—and make a well-informed judgement call. Do you have enough runway to get this big idea off the ground and create superior value? Can you beat the competition? Sustainable competitive advantage is the holy grail of business strategy, but let's be clear: sustainable competitive advantage is virtually always beyond reach. It's something you aim for, knowing full well you will never quite get there. You just keep working, adjusting to changes and finding new ways to distinguish yourself in the marketplace. Still, you do need to try to achieve some degree of longevity. Use the Assessing Competitive Advantage framework to help you determine if you're ready to take the leap and move your idea forward, or if you have a competitive disadvantage and need to scrap this idea and go after something better.

ASSESSING COMPETITIVE ADVANTAGE

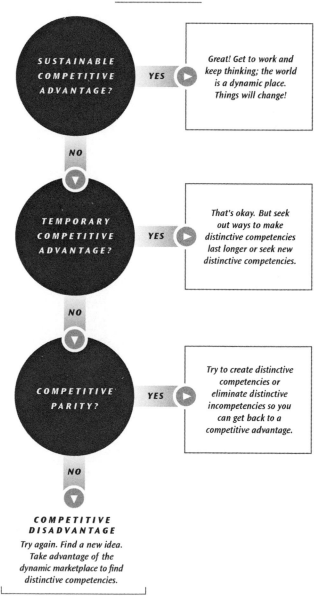

Assessing Competitive Advantage

RESOURCES

EROSION MATRIX FOR COMPETENCIES

ITEM	DISTINCTIVE COMPETENCY ⊕	ERODING FACTOR ⊖ Works against distinctive competency	LIKELIHOOD Scale of 1–10, with 10 being currently exists or certain to occur	IMPACT Scale of 1–10, with 10 having profound and significant impact on the organization	EROSION RATING Likelihood multiplied by impact

ENABLERS MATRIX FOR COMPETENCIES

DISTINCTIVE COMPETENCY ⊕	ERODING FACTOR ⊖ List those with the highest erosion ratings	ENABLING FACTOR List as many enabling factors as you can think of that may work against each eroding factor	FREQUENCY OF NEED Scale of 1–10, with 1 being rarely and 10 being daily	IMPACT OF NOT HAVING ENABLER Scale of 1–10, with 10 being a profound negative impact on the organization	ENABLING SCORE Frequency multiplied by impact

GENERAL OPERATIONAL ENABLERS 1. List all operational enablers you can think of 2. Rate frequency, impact and calculate enabling score					

GENERAL ENABLERS OF COMPETENCIES ⊕			FREQUENCY OF NEED Scale of 1–10, 1 being rarely and 10 being daily	IMPACT OF ENABLER ⊕ Scale of 1–10, with 10 being a profound positive impact	ENABLING SCORE Frequency multiplied by impact

EROSION MATRIX FOR INCOMPETENCIES

DISTINCTIVE INCOMPETENCY ⊖	ERODING FACTOR ⊕ To help overcome or defend against incompetency	LIKELIHOOD Scale of 1-10, with 10 being eroding factor currently exists or can easily be put in place	IMPACT Scale of 1–10, with 10 having profound and significant impact on the organization	EROSION RATING Likelihood multiplied by impact

ENABLERS MATRIX FOR INCOMPETENCIES

DISTINCTIVE INCOMPETENCY ⊖	ERODING FACTOR ⊕ List those with the highest erosion ratings	ENABLING FACTOR List as many enabling factors as you can think of that may support each eroding factor	FREQUENCY OF NEED Scale of 1–10, with 1 being rarely and 10 being daily	IMPACT OF NOT HAVING ENABLER ⊖ Scale of 1–10, with 10 being a profound negative impact on the organization	ENABLING SCORE Frequency multiplied by impact

GENERAL OPERATIONAL ENABLERS
1. List all ways you are enabling incompetencies in your general operations
2. Rate frequency, impact & calculate enabling score

GENERAL ENABLERS OF INCOMPETENCIES ⊖	FREQUENCY OF OCCURRENCE ⊕ Scale of 1–10, 1 being rarely and 10 being daily	IMPACT OF ENABLER ⊖ Scale of 1–10, with 10 being a profound negative impact	ENABLING SCORE Frequency multiplied by impact

SOURCES CITED

(Endnotes)

Acknowledgements

1   V-REEL is a registered trademark of David Flint.

2   Van Fleet, E.W., Van Fleet, D. D., & Flint, G. D., "Determining Market Segments for Entrepreneurial Ventures: The SPI Matrix," Journal of Applied Management and Entrepreneurship 15(1) (2010): 50-65.

3   Flint, G. D., & Van Fleet, D. D., "The Competitive Cohort: An Extension of Strategic Understanding," *Journal of Business Strategies* Vol. 28, No. 2 (2011): 97-122.

4   Cory, K. D., Flint, G. D., & Van Fleet, D. D., "V-REEL: An Improved Framework for Teaching (and Implementing) the Resource-Based View," *Journal of Strategic Management Education* 9(1) (2013): 41-56.

Chapter 1

5   Levy, Francesca and Rodkin, Jonathan, "The Bloomberg Recruiter Report: Job Skills Companies Want But Can't Get," *Bloomberg,* https://www.bloomberg.com/graphics/2015-job-skills-report/.

6   "Do economic or industry factors affect business survival?" SBA Office of Advocacy, Small Business Facts, June 2012, https://www.sba.gov/sites/default/files/Business-Survival.pdf.

7   "Startup Business Failure Rate by Industry," *Statistic Brain,* January 24, 2016, http://www.statisticbrain.com/startup-failure-by-industry/.

Chapter 2

8   Hitt, M. A, Ireland, R. D., and Hoskisson, R. E., *Strategic Management: Competitiveness and Globalization, Concepts and Cases* 12e (Boston, MA: Cengage Learning, 2008), p. 16.

9   Jethro Nededog, "How the 'Friends' cast nabbed their insane salaries of $1 million per episode," *Business Insider,* Oct. 6, 2016, http://www.businessinsider.com/how-friends-cast-got-1-million-per-episode-salary-2016-10/#all-the-circumstances-were-just-right-1

10   Rothman, Simon, "Why Uber Won: The Startup Steroid Era of Capital as Performance Enhancing Drug," *Greylock Partners,* April 20, 2016, https://news.greylock.com/why-uber-won-5598a2a66561.

11   Sonders, Mike, "These latest UBER statistics show how it's dominating Lyft," *Medium,* December 7, 2016, https://medium.com/@sm_app_intel/these-latest-uber-statistics-show-how-its-dominating-lyft-53f6b255de5e.

12   Taxicab, Limousine, & Paratransit Association, https://www.tlpa.org/.

13   *Who's Driving You,* http://www.whosdrivingyou.org/.

14   Krantz, Matt and Swartz, Jon, "IBM joins elite group of 100-year-old companies," *USA Today/Executive Suite,* June 16, 2011, http://usatoday30.usatoday.com/money/companies/management/2011-06-15-ibm-corporate-longevity_n.htm.

Chapter 3

15   Dunston, Dain, "Blockbuster: The customer owns your purpose." *Dain Dunston, The Language of Leadership,* http://daindunston.com/blockbuster-the-customer-owns-your-purpose/.

16   Ibid.

17   Bates, James, "Corner Turned, Blockbuster's New CEO Says," *Los Angeles Times,* April 8, 1998, http://articles.latimes.com/1998/apr/08/business/fi-37106.

18   Dunston, Dain, "Blockbuster: The customer owns your purpose." *Dain Dunston, The Language of Leadership,* http://daindunston.com/blockbuster-the-customer-owns-your-purpose/.

19   Ibid.

Chapter 4

20   "The QSR 50: A quick look at the top brands in quick service and fast casual," *QSR Magazine,* August 2016, https://www.qsrmagazine.com/reports/qsr50-2016-top-50-chart.

21   Nykiel, Ronald A., Handbook of Marketing Research Methodologies for Hospitality and Tourism, (New York, NY: Routledge, 2009).

22   "A lesson in customer service from Chick-fil-A President Dan Cathy," *SAS,* https://www.sas.com/en_us/insights/articles/marketing/a-lesson-in-customer-service-from-chick-fil-a.html.

23   Sauter, Michael B., Frohlich, Thomas C., and Stebbins, Samuel, "Customer Service Hall of Fame," *24/7 Wallstreet,* July 23,

2105, http://247wallst.com/special-report/2015/07/23/customer-service-hall-of-fame-2/.

24   Gillett, Rachel, "8 reasons why working at Facebook is better than working at Google," *Business Insider*, April 28, 2015, http://www.businessinsider.com/why-its-better-to-work-at-facebook-than-google-2015-4.

25   "The QSR 50: A quick look at the top brands in quick service and fast casual," *QSR Magazine*, August 2016, https://www.qsrmagazine.com/reports/qsr50-2016-top-50-chart.

26   "Our History," *Walmart.com*, http://corporate.walmart.com/our-story/our-history.

27   Ibid.

28   Ibid.

29   Ibid.

30   Ibid.

31   Hyde, Rachael , "How Walmart Model Wins with 'Everyday Low Prices'," *Investopedia*, January 18, 2015, http://www.investopedia.com/articles/personal-finance/011815/how-walmart-model-wins-everyday-low-prices.asp.

32   Ibid.

33   Oyedele, Akin and Gould, Skye, "These are the 10 biggest employers in the world," *Business Insider*, June 23, 2015, http://www.businessinsider.com/biggest-workforces-in-the-world-2015-6.

Chapter 5

34   "Yogi Berra Quotes," *Goodreads.com*, http://www.goodreads.com/author/quotes/79014.Yogi_Berra.

35   "IBM typewriter milestones," IBM.com, https://www-03.ibm.com/ibm/history/exhibits/modelb/modelb_milestone.html.

36   "The birth of the IBM PC," IBM.com, https://www-03.ibm.com/ibm/history/exhibits/pc25/pc25_birth.html.

37   Kell, John, "Hormel goes organic with latest big food acquisition," *Fortune*, May 26, 2015, http://fortune.com/2015/05/26/hormel-buys-applegate-farms/.

38   Gee, Kelsey and Haddon, Heather, "Food Giants Set Their Sights on Organic Natural Food Companies," *Wall Street Journal*, July 8, 2016, https://www.wsj.com/articles/food-giants-set-their-sights-on-organic-natural-companies-1467990819.

39   "Welcome to IBM at 100," *IBM.com*, https://www-03.ibm.com/ibm/history/ibm100/us/en/.

40   Rodgers, William, *THINK: A Biography of the Watsons and IBM* (New York, NY: Stein and Day, 1969) p. 52.

41   "IBM highlights 1885-1969," *IBM.com*, https://www-03.ibm.com/ibm/history/documents/pdf/1885-1969.pdf.

42   "Chonological history of IBM, 1930s," *IBM.com*, http://www-03.ibm.com/ibm/history/history/decade_1930.html.

43   IBM archives, 1940s, https://www-03.ibm.com/ibm/history/history/year_1940.html.

44   Wise, T.A., "I.B.M.'s $5,000,000,000 Gamble," *Fortune*, September 1966, p. 118.

45   Jackson, Joab, "The mainframe turns 50, or, why the IBM System/360 launch was the dawn of enterprise IT," *PC World*, April 7, 2014,   http://www.pcworld.com/article/2140220/the-mainframe-turns-50-or-why-the-ibm-system360-launch-was-the-dawn-of-enterprise-it.html.

46   "IBM Centennial Film: They Were There—People who changed the way the world works," *You Tube*, Jan 20, 2011, https://www.youtube.com/watch?v=XrhDaAmn5Uw.

47   Van Kralingen, Bridget, "IBM's Transformation—From Survival to Success," *Forbes*, July 7, 2010, https://www.forbes.com/2010/07/07/ibm-transformation-lessons-leadership-managing-change.html.

48   Gerstner, Jr., Louis V., *Who Says Elephants Can't Dance?: Inside IBM's Historic Turnaround*, (New York, NY: Harper Business, 2002) p. 372.

49   Tobey, Pam, "IBM Stock Performance Over 30 Years," *Washington Post*, August 27, 2013, https://www.washingtonpost.com/apps/g/page/business/ibm-stock-performance-over-30-years/416/.

50   Ginni Rometty, Ginni Rometty on the Cognitive Era, https://www.ibm.com/cognitive/ca-en/outthink/

Chapter 6

51   "The Pizza Turnaround Documentary," *PizzaTurnaround.com*, December 21, 2009, http://pizzaturnaround.com/.

52   Stone, Brad, "Steve Jobs: The Return, 1997-2011," *Bloomberg Business Week*, October 6, 2011, https://www.bloomberg.com/news/articles/2011-10-06/steve-jobs-the-return-1997-2011.

53   Abell, John C., "Aug. 6, 1997: Apple Rescued—By Microsoft," August 6, 2009, *WIRED*, https://www.wired.com/2009/08/dayintech_0806/.

54   Stone, Brad, "Steve Jobs: The Return, 1997-2011," *Bloomberg Business Week*, October 6, 2011, https://www.bloomberg.com/news/articles/2011-10-06/steve-jobs-the-return-1997-2011.

Morgan James
Speakers Group

We connect Morgan James published
authors with live and online events
and audiences who will benefit
from their expertise.